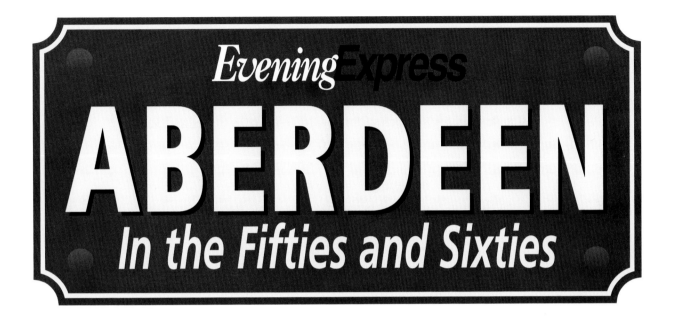

Evening Express

ABERDEEN
In the Fifties and Sixties

David Smith

breedon books
PUBLISHING

First published in Great Britain in 2001 by
The Breedon Books Publishing Company Limited
Breedon House, 3 The Parker Centre, Derby, DE21 4SZ.

ISBN 1 85983 267 9

Printed and bound by Butler & Tanner, Frome, Somerset, England.
Jacket printing by GreenShires, Leicester, England.

Contents

Acknowledgements

This book has come together with not a little help from my friends. Former colleagues, ex-council officials and retired police officers, all put their thinking caps on to turn back the years and recall not just pictures, but events and anecdotes to help me bring these two decades back to life.

My heartfelt thanks go to Duncan Smith and his staff in the library at Aberdeen Journals for all their digging to produce most of the pictures in this book.

Bruce Irvine, the printer in the photographic department, is to be congratulated for retrieving so many excellent pictures from the department's files, including numerous original glass plates, and transforming torn, tattered and faded prints into pristine pictures suitable for publication.

I am indebted to my colleague of many years, Ronnie Robertson, formerly sports editor of the *Evening Express*, whose hours of researching his personal archive of sporting facts, particularly about the Dons, has proved invaluable.

My predecessor as chief reporter and news editor at the *Evening Express*, Jimmy Lees proved a great font of information about people and events featured here.

My thanks to photographers Mike Stephen and David Sutherland for sharing their memories with me and recalling so many excellent pictures I had long forgotten.

And I should like to express my appreciation to Ron Fiddes for the pictures from his collection on everything from school outings to sports teams which appear on these pages.

Without all these people and the memories of a few others, the compilation of this book would have proved a much more difficult task, and would not have been the pleasure that it has. For their support and input I am extremely grateful.

Introduction

WHEN I undertook to put together a book on the Fifties and Sixties I could never have realised just how much I had forgotten about those 20 eventful years in the history of the North-East. Those two decades took up my entire schooldays right through into my early years as a reporter for the *Evening Express* and *The Press and Journal* in Banff in 1963 and 1964 and at Broad Street in Aberdeen until Aberdeen Journals flitted to Mastrick in 1970.

Not until I started archiving the hidden treasure of black and white photographs in the library of Aberdeen Journals at Mastrick, did the memories of those two decades come flooding back. Thanks to the work, often in difficult and challenging circumstances, of photographers like Ian Hardie, Jack Cryle, Gordon Bissett, David Sutherland, John Gallicker, Jim Love, Charlie Flett and Mike Stephen, a photographic history of Aberdeen and the North-East has been captured for ever in the form of hundreds of pictures, many of which they probably thought would never see the light of day again.

Sifting through the pictures, mostly of Aberdeen, has been like taking a journey back through time. George Street and St Nicholas Street before the days of the St Nicholas Centre and Bon-Accord Centre. Union Street when the trams rattled noisily back and forth from the Bridge of Don, Bridge of Dee and Hazlehead. Shops we'd almost forgotten like The Equitable, Isaac Benzie, the George Street Woolie's, and, of course, the Co-opie in Loch Street. The statue of Queen Victoria – 'the auld Queen' – when it was moved from the corner of St Nicholas Street to Queen's Cross.

How sad, for example, that Aberdeen's superb dog racing stadium at Bridge of Dee had to disappear to make way for a supermarket. Particularly sad for my dad, Bill Smith, who had been a bookie there since before World War Two. In my final year at Aberdeen Academy, he decided I should accompany him to the Saturday night race meetings to learn to be his floorman – an experience which convinced me I was not cut out to be a turf commission agent.

No one in Aberdeen should forget the contribution made to the health of women and children by Sir Dugald Baird, the renowned obstetrician, who championed the birth pill, abortion on social grounds, and pioneered screening for cervical cancer. And no one deserved more the honour of becoming a Freeman of Aberdeen in 1966. It was particularly appropriate that his wife, Lady May, should share the accolade for her work in health and civic affairs – a historic occasion because they were the first husband and wife to be so honoured by the city.

Without a doubt Aberdeen's best loved medical practitioner was Dr Mary Esslemont who had surgeries in the west-end and Torry. A gynaecologist at the free dispensary in the Guestrow, she became the first woman president of the Medico-Chirurgical Society in 1957. She was the first woman chairman of the British Medical Association, later becoming a life president, having been elected a fellow in 1959. She became a fellow of the Royal College of General Practitioners in 1969 and received a CBE in 1955. A JP she served on the University Court throughout the Fifties and Sixties, until 1974 and was awarded the freedom of the city in 1981.

The health of Aberdeen was never more in the spotlight than in 1964 when the city became isolated from the rest of the world following an outbreak of typhoid fever. For five weeks the eyes of the world were on the city where 400 people were quarantined in hospital wards. The city's medical officer of health, Dr Ian McQueen announced no one should leave the city and no one should enter while the epidemic raged. Only when the Queen visited the city to declare the epidemic over, did people recognise Aberdeen was a safe place to visit again.

In 1963 Aberdeen became the unlikely setting for a milestone in criminal history when Henry Burnett became the last man to hang in Scotland. Crowds, including my father and I, lined the walls of Craiginches Prison on the morning of the hanging in 1963. No one had been executed in the city for more than 100 years. I include the first in-depth interview with the then prison chaplain, Rev John Dickson, about the days leading up to the hanging which he witnessed and which still troubles him today.

Six years after that shameful event, the North-East

was rocked by the most sensational murder trial the North-East had ever known – the Garvie trial. With its strong sexual element, the murder of wealthy Mearns farmer and amateur pilot, Maxwell Garvie, by his beautiful wife, Sheila, and her lover, Brian Tevendale, generated huge crowds outside the High Court in Aberdeen.

The slaying of two children in Aberdeen within less than two years sparked the biggest manhunt the city had ever seen. Six-year-old June Cruickshank was killed near her Printfield home while on an errand in 1961. Seven-year-old George Forbes of Justice Street died on an allotment at Castlehill. Both had their throats cut. The hunt for the killer ended three years later with the arrest of James Oliphant who was later sent to Carstairs for life.

Tragedy of a different kind befell the families of seamen from the North and North-East throughout the Fifties and Sixties. In the early Fifties, all but one of the crew of the Fraserburgh Lifeboat lost their lives when it was overwhelmed by a huge wave at the entrance to the harbour.

In 1965 Aberdeen was devastated by the loss of the Aberdeen trawler, Blue Crusader, which disappeared with her crew of 13 after sailing into a storm off Orkney. The generous people of Aberdeen raised more than £25,000 for their grief-stricken families.

The decade was to end with one of the greatest tragedies ever to hit the seafaring community in Scotland – the Longhope Lifeboat disaster – which has particularly poignant memories for me as I was assigned to cover the story for the *Evening Express*. Seven brave Orkney crewmen from the island of Hoy died when their vessel was overwhelmed by heavy seas while going to the aid of a cargo vessel which had run aground on the island of South Ronaldsay on the night of March 17, 1969.

Among the other pictures of drama at sea featured in these pages, one of the most memorable is of the Aberdeen trawler, Red Crusader, running from a Danish Navy vessel which had tried to arrest it on the high seas. Accused of illegal fishing in Faroese waters, Skipper 'Typhoon' Ted Wood remained true to his formidable reputation when he made a run for it rather than risk a massive fine. He did not stop even after the Danish captain fired on his vessel.

If ever there was a time of change in Aberdeen and the North-East then this was it. From dark post-war days when we were still rationed for certain items – especially sweeties – through the Swinging Sixties and the arrival of the North Sea oil boom, the city underwent incredible change and so did its people.

Familiar buildings were swept away, and whole new housing estates were born. Mastrick and Northfield were first, started and completed in the Fifties and Sixties. South Sheddocksley and Denmore quickly followed. Restrictions on the private sector were lifted in the early Fifties and the pace of private housing increased dramatically.

Aberdeen's first multi-storey flats were built for the council by Alexander Hall Ltd in Ashgrove in 1960 and this form of construction dominated right through the Sixties. Families living in appalling slum conditions in ghettos like Black's Buildings and Castlehill Barracks were gradually moved out into new council homes more in tune with the 20th century.

As the population shifted away from the city centre, public transport needs changed dramatically, leading to the demise of Aberdeen's much loved tram system.

The Aberdeen District Tramways Company opened in 1874, the first horse tramway service running from the North Church on King Street to Queen's Cross and from St Nicholas Street to Causwayend. The company was taken over by the town council in 1898. By 1901 the expanding service reached the beach. The tramways reached the limit of the system in the 1920s. The construction of the new housing estates in the Fifties at Northfield, Mastrick and Kincorth spelled the end of the line for the trams and culminated in them being ceremoniously torched at the beach – again recorded for posterity by our photographers.

The day of the bus had arrived, and the car was becoming king. More city centre car parking became essential leading to multi-storey car parks like the Shiprow becoming a feature of the landscape. As the economy of the city improved new shops opened up in George Street, St Nicholas Street and Union Street as well as on the outskirts. The day of the supermarket had arrived.

The city's skyline changed dramatically with the advent of high rise flats, and new landmarks like St Nicholas House, Norco in George Street and the Lang Stracht Hotel sparked considerable debate as to their architectural merits.

In sport the city achieved greatness in football, with the Dons winning the double in 1954 – the first Dons team ever to clinch the Scottish League championship. Sadly, gone, but not forgotten, the magnificent Archie Glen's finest moment came when he scored the goal which sealed the history-making result. Also in that dream team were the legendary Paddy Buckley, who once drove Jock Stein to rip off his shirt in sheer frustration, Golden Boy Harry Yorston and the unforgettable Graham Leggatt.

One of Aberdeen's greatest sporting heroes, Ian Black, is remembered here for the glory he brought to Aberdeen and Scotland in a glittering swimming career, which ended when he was just 20-years-old. In the years up to the 1960 Rome Olympics where failure to secure a medal heralded his retirement, Ian was the darling of the city, and the nation which showered him with honours.

Others sporting greats whose pictures you'll find here are cricketers Rohan Kanhai and George Youngson, golfers Sandy Pirie and Harry Bannerman, and rugby ace Ian McRae. And what boxing fan could forget the superb Johnny Kidd whose reign of triumph lasted through the Fifties into the Sixties.

Images of days gone by enrich these pages. From the Timmer Market to the Turriff Show, our photographers were there to record faces and events that will live forever. Characters, of course, abound, some of whom I knew personally, others only by reputation. As a five-year-old going to Woodside School, my day would not have been complete without a visit to Andy McKessock's glory hole shop in Great Northern Road. Thanks to local historian Andy, the story of Woodside has been recorded for posterity.

Few of my generation will have forgotten that amazing entrepreneur, Councillor Tom Scott Sutherland, after whom the Scott Sutherland School of Architecture was named. Born in Walker Road, Torry, he was brought up in Ferryhill and later Burns Road. Among the cinemas he designed and built were the Regent, later the Odeon which closed its doors for the last time in June of this year, the Majestic, the City in George Street, and the Astoria at Kittybrewster. He built the Amicable building in Union Street, and renovated the Tivoli theatre. As housing convenor he pursued an active slum clearing and building programme at Hilton, Powis, Woodside and Kaimhill

and planned the Kincorth housing estate. His fortune was used to establish the school of architecture.

I well remember old G.R. McIntosh, the doughty Aberdeen Labour councillor who liked nothing better than to visit our Broad Street offices to discuss civic affairs with reporters like John Dunbar, Ethel Simpson or Hector McSporran. And heads never failed to be turned by the beautiful Susan Jones, daughter of Professor R.V. Jones, the famous wartime boffin and intelligence expert, who took the Miss Scotland title three times before going on to become a finalist in the Miss Universe contest in Miami in 1961.

Shopping in the Fifties and Sixties was a joy in stores like Isaac Benzie, Watt & Grant, Esslemont & Macintosh and the Equitable where I bought my first record, a 78 of Duane Eddy playing Peter Gunn. Their customer base extended as far away as Peterhead, Banff, Speyside and Orkney and Shetland. And everyone knew their Co-op divi number. From its Gallowgate base it expanded throughout the city. The Sixties ended with the opening of Norco House in George Street, considered by many to be the ugliest building ever in Aberdeen.

Life changed dramatically in 1954 when television came to Aberdeen with the BBC starting transmission to the North-East. The television age really arrived in 1961 when Grampian TV started transmissions creating new personalities like June Imrie, Douglas Kynoch, Jimmy Spankie and John Mearns.

The citizens of Aberdeen in the Sixties became aware of a growing cultural diversity. The first Chinese restaurant, The Bamboo, opened in Union Street in 1961 and was followed by new hotels, restaurants, café bars and gambling casinos. Curry, however, was still regarded as foreign muck to be avoided at all costs

All of these and many like them are part of the history and fabric of Aberdeen and deserve to be remembered. Browse through the pictures we have put together here and you may well find people and places that mean something to you. Brothers, sisters, uncle, aunts, even grandparents you may have never seen. Perhaps you'll find your old house that was swept away to make way for the new Aberdeen. Your old school may be featured or the firm you once worked for.

Whatever the memories these pictures may evoke, it has been my great pleasure to dust them down and bring them back to life.

Changing Times

Old meets new in Woodside on Great Northern Road near the Haudagain roundabout. Few remember the misery of the families who lived in tents and temporary shacks on the two Haudagain fields off Great Northern Road. With no water supply, the tenants lived in the rat-infested muddy fields until the town council moved them in 1936 to a variety of temporary accommodation at the King Street Barracks, Aberdeen jute works, Castlehill Barracks and the Torry Battery. The buildings in this 1963 picture represent three periods. On the left, early 20th century tenements. Centre – modern Fyfestone blocks of flats built by Aberdeen Town Council and right, the much older houses of the type in which poet Lord Byron stayed with his old nurse at 719 Great Northern Road in the last decade of the 18th century.

Another Aberdeen pub passes out of private hands into the empire of the brewing giants. In September 1965, The Silver Slipper, and Cinderella Lounges, in Rosemount Viaduct, which opened in 1960, were sold by Henry Gilbert to Scottish Brewers Ltd.

Long since demolished this magnificent block of flats formed the corner of Great Western Road and Hammerfield Avenue just west of Anderson Drive when this picture was taken in 1967.

Sandilands Drive, in July 1958 a deprived area beset by social and health problems. A model scheme when it opened in the late Thirties, many of its first residents came from city slums. The first tenants had their own gardens and people would come for Sunday walks to look at the flowers in the neat gardens. But then came decline, with residents complaining of council indifference to their plight. Dampness, vandalism, health problems and unemployment were among the area's worst problems creating the worst area of urban deprivation in the city. The 416 houses in the area, including, Ferrier Crescent, Ferrier Gardens, Barron Street, Marquis Road, Western Road and part of Great Northern Road were later re-named Fersands and became the first housing area in the North of Scotland to benefit from the government's Urban Aid Scheme to improve deprived areas.

The multi-storey development at the Shiprow was well under way in March 1967 when this picture was taken. The towering glass and concrete building, fronting on to Castle Street would become the Grandfare supermarket with individual shops below. At the rear, facing the harbour, is the new multi-storey car park.

The *Evening Express* took to the air in a small aircraft in July 1963, to capture this fabulous shot of the city's unique Rosemount Square. Bathed in the warm sun, the square is surrounded by Northfield Place, Leadside Road, Richmond Street, Rosemount Viaduct and Kintore Place.

A cloud of lime rises as the gable end of a building falls as part of the demolition of old properties in Broad Street in 1967 to make way for Aberdeen Corporation's new administrative headquarters. St. Nicholas House is becoming recognisable as the cladding and windows go around the massive structure.

Trams as far as the eye can see. This impressive aerial shot of Union Street looking west to Holburn Junction gives an unusual birds-eye view of the city's main thoroughfare as it looked in the Fifties. Three different kinds of trams as well as single and double decker buses can be seen in the picture and all had conductors to take the fares.

This picture shows in the most dramatic way how badly needed a new city centre shopping area was in 1959. Narrow pavements fail to contain the crowds of shoppers while people dodge cars and buses to cross from shop to shop.

Long before shopping malls came on the scene, Aberdeen city centre in 1963 was a maze of shops and local department stores. This photograph is taken from the corner of Correction Wynd looking on to St Nicholas Street and into the Netherkirkgate where the Wallace Tower can be seen on the right before it was moved stone by stone to Tillydrone. That year discussions were under way in the nearby Town House about the need to modernise the busy corner as well as further up George Street. Our picture shows just how run down some of the buildings were. Due to uncertainty over what should happen in the future it would be the advent of the oil industry a few years later and the subsequent boom that led to the city's comprehensive development plan swinging into action and a stream of public inquiries which culminated in the city centre we know today.

After 56 years, Robert Stephen's second-hand bookshop closed down in 1967 after serving generations of Aberdonians. Opened in the Upperkirkgate in 1911 by Robert Stephen, it had been carried on since 1929 by his daughter, Mary, who decided to retire due to ill health. The 17th century building was formerly a town house whose sundials still protrude from its gables next to Drum's Lane.

The new high rise flats at Hazlehead stand proudly in the June sunshine in 1969 with the buildings of the new Hazlehead Academy, replacement for Aberdeen Academy, nearing completion behind them. The holiday caravan site at Hazlehead Park is just to the left of the school.

Stockethill takes shape at a rate of knots in October 1968. The pre-fabs have been removed and in their place go up new houses, including four multi-storey blocks. On the right of the picture North Anderson Drive sweeps past with Mastrick laid out behind. The Rosehill pre-fabs were the first to go in Aberdeen followed by 18 at Girdleness.

Horses graze contentedly in a pleasant pastoral scene which was about to disappear for ever in fast-changing Aberdeen in 1969. The city's new Raeden housing development was going up on the former farm land bounded by North Anderson Drive, Midstocket Road, Westburn Road and Beechwood School. A year earlier Raeden Farm was pulled down to make way for the new development which was completed in the spring of 1970.

A magnificent view from the air of Tillydrone in September 1969 with the crook of the River Don on the left, and its new high rises dominating the foreground.

The old meets the new – a stunning view of the rebuilt Wallace Tower with the new high rises at Tillydrone nearing completion behind it in December 1967.

A fine view from the air of Aberdeen's pre-fabs in 1966. These homes at Nigg are bounded by Hillview Road on the left of the picture and Wellington Road leading to Nigg Brae.

Three generation of the new Mastrick's residents make their way home from the shops with Mastrick Land towering behind them. The high rise formed the hub of the new community.

Down to earth with a bump and traffic is diverted down Abbotswell Road in February 1968 after subsidence forced the closure of Nigg Brae.

The Aberdeen Town Council housing schemes of Mastrick and Summerhill expand fast behind the imposing grounds of Woodend Hospital in April 1964.

One of Aberdeen's most notorious slums, Black's Buildings, at the Denburn, under demolition in September 1958.

BBC 2 comes to Aberdeen – but this was the price the folk in North-field had to pay. The giant aerial slowly rises beside the old one at Granitehill in 1966 to allow BBC 2 programmes to reach the city. When the third channel was beamed out from the new station at Durris, in 1967, it was through transmitting facilities on the new Northfield mast.

On their way to the shops these two ladies take a short cut to Union Street via Jack's Brae in 1966. Familiar to generations few know who Jack was. The street dates back to the mid 18th century and council records from 1758 reveal: 'The council approves the feuing out of that piece of ground… the west part whereof to be feud out by John Jack, manufacturer at Gilcomstone at the yearly value of eight shillings sterling of yearly feu duty.' Jack's Brae, like many streets in the Gilcomston area, all but disappeared in the slum clearances which started in the Thirties. Only a meal mill at the top of the Brae remained until it suffered the same fate in 1984.

Old fashioned gas street lamps are in sharp contrast to the television age in Footdee's North Square in 1964. Neighbours in Aberdeen's quaintest community enjoy a chat in front of the low ceilinged cottages similar to those found in many fishing villages throughout the North-East.

Marischal Street, Aberdeen in 1969. Our picture shows the sign outside the offices of George Kemp, Turf Commission Agent, better known to followers of horse and dog racing in Aberdeen, as Dodie Kemp the bookie. The buildings from 42 to 48 Marischal Street were designed by William Smith – Sink 'em Smith – around 1780. He was the father of John Smith, City Architect, and grandfather of William Smith, builder of Balmoral Castle.

Many Aberdeen tenements still looked like this in the Fifties. Though it looks straight out of the Thirties, this was a downstairs flat in Granton Place in 1959.

How the heart of Aberdeen could have looked if students at Aberdeen School of Architecture in 1966 had got their way. This revolutionary design was how the pre-final year students saw the area bounded by Union Street, Bridge Street, Guild Street, and Market Street. The plan did away with all the buildings in the area replacing them with tiers of shops in Union Street with offices and houses above, a bowling rink, ice skating rink in Market Street and a new repertory theatre between Guild Street and Union Street. They also planned a multi-storey car park in Bridge Street, a new market building and an elevated inner ring road above Guild Street. Our picture shows delegates attending the 50th convention of the Royal Incorporation of Architects in Scotland.

End of an era – the Gordon Highlanders Club at 151 King Street, Aberdeen in 1964 after it was closed and sold to Aberdeen University, despite strenuous efforts by members to save it. More than 350 ex-Gordons signed a petition to keep it going for another year but financial constraints sealed the club's fate. The former County Hotel was acquired by the club as temporary premises in 1922.

It may have been the Swinging Sixties but there were still streets in Aberdeen illuminated at night by gas. In August 1961 leerie Harry Robertson was still shinning up ladders to maintain the Victorian-style lamps with their warm, eerie glow. Harry is pictured here at work on one of the city's 4,204 lamps still in use at the time.

Water workers in 1961 still wore uniforms and peaked caps. Here William Buyers of Aberdeen Corporation Water Department tests a water meter before it was put back into use. Meters had to be two-and-a-half per cent accurate before they could be re-installed.

Just a small tap – on a small tap. The official stamp of approval was punched on every tap that passed the rigorous test at Aberdeen Corporation Water Department's workshops at Cattofield Place. Here George Insch bestows the sign of approval on a tap for use on a washing machine in August 1961.

Farmers shelter from the rain under the wooden balcony of Aberdeen Mart at Kittybrewster in November 1960. The mart's wooden, pillared front, was unique in Aberdeen, matched by the row of quaint, wood fronted shops opposite.

A resident of the model lodging house as Provost Skene's House was in this Thirties picture warms himself by the centuries old fireplace.

It was only right that the Queen Mother should have been invited to officially open the restored Provost Skene's House in Aberdeen's Guest Row on the last day of September 1953. For no one had played a more prominent part in bringing the dream of restoration to fruition. In the critical period in 1938 when the building was threatened with demolition she used her considerable influence to save the historic 16th-century building. The demolish-or-preserve battle followed a recommendation to the town council that a new town house should be erected in the cleared area opposite Marischal College. On a visit to the house in 1938, at that time a model lodging house, the Queen as she was then, expressed concern for its future to Lord Provost Watt, who was in favour of retaining it. At the official opening, the Queen Mother said the restoration was a dream she had long cherished.

Formerly Cumberland House, the 16th-century Provost Skene's House in the Guest Row, as it looked before restoration work which was completed in 1953. In 1745 the Duke of Cumberland stayed there while pursuing Bonnie Prince Charlie, the Young Pretender who was in retreat after failing to invade England and win back the throne.

In 1951 Co-opie coal kept the home fires burning all over Aberdeen. Here Northern Co-operative Society lorries line up to take coal straight off Aberdeen's famous coal boat, the *Thrift*, at Aberdeen Harbour.

Rows of trawlers line up at Point Law as they for wait their crews to return to sea at the height of Aberdeen's success as a major UK fishing port in 1958.

Man-made ice creates a wintry scene at Aberdeen Fish Market in December 1967. Fish market porters unload tons of top quality cod, haddock and other species from seiners and trawlers from ports including Peterhead, Banff, Buckie, Macduff, Gardenstown and Aberdeen.

Look, there are boats at the bottom of our street! These trawlers make a striking feature in this remarkable shot taken in 1964 from the opposite side of Aberdeen harbour showing one of Aberdeen's steepest braes running up from Sinclair Road and Abbey Road to Victoria Road and the heart of Torry.

Trawlerman's son, Councillor Tom Scott Sutherland gets a helping hand aboard the new Aberdeen trawler, *George Craig* in September 1958. Despite having one leg and having to get around with a crutch and stick the Aberdeen tycoon made a memorable trip on the trawler, writing about his experiences in *The Press and Journal*. The number 13, Tom always said played an important part in his life. The son of a trawler deckhand was born on the 13th day of January 1899, set himself on the road to tycoon status at 13 Bridge Street, and died on June 13, 1963. His death brought to a close a career equal to any carved out by a son of Aberdeen. The Robert Gordon's College pupil, who lost a leg in a childhood accident, went on to climb to the top of the ladder of success. He set up business as an architect at 13 Bridge Street and quickly spotted suitable sites for housing developments. The result was the numerous Sutherland bungalows in various parts of the city, particularly Broomhill and Mannofield. He acquired an interest in Moore's Medicinal products Ltd in London, ultimately buying out his colleagues and transferring the business to Aberdeen. He bought a distillery, promoted companies and held numerous directorships of companies, including two with film studios producing live and animated programmes and advertising films for commercial television. The author of two amusing books the hard-hitting anti-socialist became a town councillor in 1934. Among his benefactions was the gift to his old school of Garthdee House and 20 acres of policies for the school of architecture which bears his name. A keen Dons fan he twice made unsuccessful bids to take over Aberdeen Football Club. A conjurer and founder member of Aberdeen Magical Society, he was for 16 years, until 1958, a director of the Tivoli. One of his last deals was the purchase in 1963 of two of Aberdeenshire's biggest and best equipped dairy farms at Westerton and Easterton, Rothienorman, which he leased back to their former owner, Maitland Mackie jun.

Ready for sea – and anything it can throw at them – these determined-looking seamen are the 1963 crew of Aberdeen Lifeboat. On the right of the picture is the familiar figure of coxwain Leo Clegg.

War hero, sculptor, teacher, sailor, lifeboatman – Leo Clegg, coxwain of Aberdeen Lifeboat was all these things. Leo had barely started his art training when World War Two broke out and he found himself on a Navy gunboat, MGB 307, which he later commanded until the end of the war. For his part on the greatest raid of World War Two – the attack on the submarine pens at St. Nazaire – he won the DSC. While lecturing at Gray's School of Art, Leo sailed his own boat out of Aberdeen for many years. In 1960 he became cox of the Aberdeen Lifeboat, sailing straight into a storm. The governors of Robert Gordon's Colleges asked him to resign but he refused. They finally relented and Leo's career as a lifeboatman continued until 1969 when he moved to live in a croft at Methlick. Latterly head of the sculpture and ceramics department at Gray's he died aged just 59 in 1980 survived by his wife, Thora, three daughters and two sons.

The magnificent lead and glass frontage of A. & W. Alexander's butcher's and fishmonger's shop at Holburn Junction in 1962.

Anyone who lost a button in Aberdeen knew just where to go to find a match. In 1960 Maxwells occupied a huge section of the upper hall at Aberdeen's New Market and along its range of stalls, shoppers could get anything from a box of Quality Street to a button for any occasion.

Staff of the Northern Co-operative Society Drapery department are the epitome of sartorial elegance as they pose for the *Evening Express* in April 1961.

This giant figure standing two storeys high on top of the canopy outside Isaac Benzies in Aberdeen's George Street was advertising the popular department store's 71st anniversary celebrations. The gala week featured not only bargains but competitions, heavily advertised in colour in the *Evening Express*.

Aberdeen's 'Mr Memory' of music, John Wood, was a much respected figure at the record counter of Bruce Miller's in George Street. John worked for the music seller for 60 years, building up an encyclopaedic knowledge of the 40,000 record titles and catalogue numbers in stock. During World War Two, while serving in the RAF, John often worked in the store while on leave. A single man, John, who was an elder of Albion St Paul's church, died in 1991.

The unmistakable frontage of the Northern Co-operative Society's headquarters in the Gallowgate in 1961.

One of the most familiar shop fronts for decades, in Aberdeen, Bruce Miller & Co in George Street. Two gents admire the radiograms and radios on display in one window while musical instruments fill the other window. Since the beginning of the century the firm was synonymous with George Street. On May 8, 1900 it became the first music shop in Scotland and only the third in Britain to be awarded the agency for the new flat gramophone records being issued by the His Master's Voice Company. The company remained in George Street until 1984 when it moved to Union Street.

A motorist stops by the newly re-opened Tourist Information kiosk at the Bridge of Dee in May 1959. With posters advertising music in Union Terrace Gardens, motor racing at Edzell and the Royal Highland Show, the assistant in the kiosk had plenty to offer visitors that summer.

Blue skies and golden sands – that was how Aberdeen optimistically presented itself as Scotland's top holiday resort in 1955.

All the day's news was there on the billboards fronting the old newsagent's kiosk outside the Beach Baths in September 1959. In those days the *Scottish Daily Express* was at its peak and no fewer than five of the billboards proclaim its news and promotions. Few worried about the health risks associated with smoking in those days and the kiosk is liberally plastered with ads for Players cigarettes. However Donald's Ice Cream and Hay's Lemonade just manage to get a mention.

Swimmers enjoy a dip in the pool at Aberdeen's Beach Baths, which by the end of the Sixties, was looking and feeling its age. The pool closed just two years into the Seventies.

After a mere 10 years in existence, Aberdeen Lads Club building was demolished to make way for the long-delayed Mounthooly roundabout development. The Hutcheon Street premises cost £35,000 to build in 1964, but seven years on it became clear they would have to go because of the vital inner ring road plans. The new roundabout was the city's biggest, covering two-and-a-half acres. The lads club moved to Tillydrone.

A year after it was planted, Aberdeen's first garden for the blind in Victoria Park was in full bloom, and full scent. The occasion, in September 1965, was marked by a special ceremony. Here Norman Milne, who played a major role in raising funds for the fragrant garden, and his guide dog, Jenny, are led into the garden by Madame Isabel Murray, watched by a crowd of several hundred.

The spring of 1964 saw the opening of Scotland's first garden for the blind. And nowhere could have been more appropriate than the Victoria Park. Because it was Aberdeen's first public park of its kind. Our picture shows Mr & Mrs Bob Reid reading the braille inscription identifying the plants in the sweet-smelling garden. At the time Bob was in his 23rd year as chairman of the Aberdeen branch of the National League of the Blind.

In 1952 an early Spring run of salmon brought big catches to all the salmon fishing stations on the east coast of Scotland. Here Robert Fiddes holds two 30lb salmon, part of an astonishing catch of more than 2,000 fish in a 30-week season. Earning less than £10 a week, the fishermen were on an end of season bonus per 100 fish caught. In just two days they made half their usual bonus!

Salmon fishermen prepare for the start of the 1954 season at Newtonhill. Here David Cargill (right) and Robert Fiddes splice the leader ropes holding the nets in position at sea. During the Fifties the advent of nylon leader ropes and nets was hailed as a major breakthrough in the fishing industry. It resulted in much less damage to the nets due to their ability to expand and contract, making them much more able to contend with the ravages of the sea.

A lifetime behind the bar of one of Aberdeen's oldest howfs came to an end in 1965 for genial Tom Summers. Tom, who took over the Torry Bar in Old Torry, in 1936, is pictured here with customers, left to right, W. Adam, R. Windgrove and J. Walker after he announced his decision to retire. The pub was the local for generations of fishermen and old salts who'd come ashore after a life at sea.

One of Aberdeen's last post-war taxi owner-drivers, William Thain of Mounthooly pictured as he waits to pick up a fare in the city centre in April 1957.

In February 1968 all taxi drivers in Aberdeen had to wear this badge. Its use was written into the hackney carriage by-laws following discussions between proprietors, operators and magistrates.

One of the North-East's greatest characters also became one of its benefactors in 1967. Mr Jimmy Nicol, of Bogentoy, Portlethen, announced he was buying Stonehaven's biggest hotel – to give it away. The well-known breeder and judge of beef cattle, and self-taught financial wizard bought the 37-bedroom Bay Hotel and promptly handed it over to the Church of Scotland for an old folks home, though not without opposition. Approval for change of use was strongly opposed within Stonehaven Town Council and finally went through on a four to three vote. Jimmy, who laughingly referred to himself as a 'poor old body of a crofter' later became one of the home's first residents after moving out of the but and ben that had been his home for many years.

A vendor sells another copy of the tabloid *Evening Express* from his stance at the corner of Broad Street and Union Street in 1951.

A superb study of a small boat fisherman enjoying the early morning sunshine at Stonehaven Harbour before heading for sea in 1963.

Buchan loon Bill Gibb graduated from the Royal College of Art to take the London fashion scene by storm. The farmer's son quickly became a world famous designer numbering stars like Twiggy among his clients. Here he makes final adjustments to one of his creations worn by model Wendy Dicker in February 1967.

A couple of Teddy Boys play it cool in Aberdeen in 1955. The draped jackets, shawl and velvet collars, and Tony Curtis hairstyle with a DA at the back were obligatory. The 'Ted' on the left is sporting the correct shoes – thick crepe-soled boppers were a must.

She enjoys a puff on her pipe while her companion takes the weight off his feet. This pair of travelling folk, their meagre belongings stacked in an old pram, were photographed in 1954 on the Aberdeen-Tarland road. The old battledress suggest he may have been an old soldier who'd opted for life on the open road.

Last orders gentlemen please. Bar staff pull the ultimate pints and fill the glasses for the last time at the tiny Wallace Tower Bar before it closed for good in January 1963. The tower survived the redevelopment of St Nicholas Street being removed and rebuilt stone by numbered stone at Tillydrone.

Mr Woodside, Andy McKessock, with the vast collection of local history he amassed over the years. Andy made it his business to build up a comprehensive people's record of the area in the face of impending change. He took cine films and photographs of views and landmarks he knew would one day be lost to future generations. His 'glory hole' shop in Great Northern Road was a mecca for kids from Hilton and Woodside who loved going to his shop for their packets of Imps, smoking cany and liquorice sticks to make their favourite drink, Black Sugar Aley.

A beaming chimney sweep, complete with traditional lum hat, hopes he won't get the brush off as he waits to give a bride a good luck kiss outside Greyfriars Church.

Never mind Aberdeen on a flag day – at a time when they were normally full, these attendants in the Guest Row car park view acres of empty parking spaces on the day a sixpenny parking charge was imposed by the town council in December 1963.

Street entertainer David Stewart with his accordion was a familiar figure on the streets of Aberdeen. Pictured here in 1958, David spent his entire life as a street entertainer until he died aged 55 in 1963.

Plodding on – a very shaggy horse leaves Aberdeen Harbour and makes its way into South Market Street with another heavy load in 1968.

Late morning in Aberdeen's West-End in January 1962 and milk is being delivered in the time-honoured way. Near the end of his round, a milkman from Kennerty's Dairy stops outside a house in Forest Avenue near Great Western Road to leave a crate of milk. The cash bag over his shoulder indicates he is also collecting his weekly payments from his regular customers.

Mick the pony was a familiar sight at Aberdeen Fish Market in the Sixties. The carter is Bill Junor who delivered sawdust and wood shavings to the fish houses for curing the fish. Bill is pictured here making his way along Riverside Drive to the fish houses under the Arches at the bottom of South College Street in October 1964.

Buses and cars squeeze past each other as workmen lift the tram lines and cobbles in Union Street in June 1958.

As Aberdeen spawned new post-war housing estates in the Fifties, the era of the tram was passing. Gradually, the tram lines came up and buses replaced the old rattlers throughout the decade. Here the last tram to Mannofield gets a big send-off on March 3, 1951.

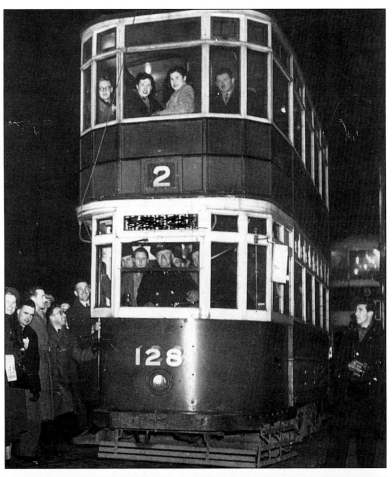

November 19, 1955 and the last tram to Woodside brings out the crowds for a fond farewell at Market Street. It would be another three years before the last tram would rattle over the cobbles in Aberdeen.

Two firemen keep a wary eye on the flames which consume the last trams ever to run over the cobbles in Aberdeen. The trams make a poignant, yet historic, picture as they are put to the torch at the beach in 1958.

Home for around 200 men down on their luck, Aberdeen Corporation Lodging House in East North Street, otherwise known as the Model Lodging House, was better known to generations of Aberdonians as The Modeller. All sorts lived there – youngsters in their 20s, pensioners in their 80s, hard-working men, workshy men. For many, drink was their downfall, some of them 'feakie' drinkers, seeking oblivion through the meths bottle. Men of all ranks passed through its doors, from ex-military men to policemen and professional men. Some lived there for more than 30 years. Our picture, taken in 1961, presents a grim picture of a Victorian-style institution, which, to its residents, was the only alternative to sleeping rough on the streets.

Lunchtime in the dining room at Aberdeen Corporation Lodging house in November 1961, and residents help themselves from the pot on the stove. The men sat on benches and ate from long tables. Dustbins stood at the table ends to receive any left-overs.

Easy does it, Your Majesty. An engineer makes sure Queen Victoria is comfy on the rear of a low loader, before making the journey from her old resting place at the corner of St Nicholas Street to Queen's Cross in January 1964.

Workmen and engineers put the finishing touches to the enthroning of Queen Victoria at her new home on the roundabout at Queen's Cross in January 1964. The spire of Queen's Cross Church makes a superb backdrop.

By 1969 it was clear to Aberdeen Corporation that the Victoria Bridge, built over the River Dee in 1881, was no longer coping with the traffic crossing from the harbour to Torry. A 1965 report showed traffic was 20 per cent above the level for which it had been designed. Our picture shows the site investigations being carried out with a view to creating what turned out to be the Queen Elizabeth 11 bridge further upstream.

No tumble dryers at Skene in 1964. Here a housewife hopes for a drying wind as she hangs out her washing at the rear of the former church which is her home while her children play nearby.

Plenty of hand-dug peat to keep the homes fires burning at Skene in 1964.

A magnificent view of the Turriff Show taken from the air in August 1968.

Ploughing as their fathers and forefathers had done before them at Charleston, Nigg, in 1969.

Gourdon fishermen re-invent the use for the baby's pram in April 1964 – to transport their baited lines to their boats.

The new £30,000 post office on Stonehaven's Allardice Street is officially opened in March 1968 by Provost John H. Stewart. Minutes after the opening, the previous building at Beachgate, some 50 yards to the south, closed for the last time after 69 valuable years of service to the community.

No traffic lights at the junction of Schoolhill and George Street in 1959, and a quiet day for the policeman on point duty.

A bustling Banchory High Street pictured in 1966. No Sunday outing from Aberdeen would have been complete without a visit to D'Agostino's for a delicious slider or cone.

Without today's huge volumes of traffic, the Woodside Fountain presents a scene of almost rural tranquility in March 1968. Small shops, tenements, churches and my first school, Woodside Primary, made for a thriving community. A wide variety of stores on Great Northern Road made shopping easy and the local chip shops did a roaring trade every night.

Extensive alterations and improvements gave a new look to the shopping experience at Esslemont & Macintosh in Union Street in September 1962. The entrance arcade and ground floor were given an impression of added spaciousness, while clever planning provided considerably more floor space.

Housed in two of the handsomest buildings in Union Street, that great survivor of the retail revolution in Aberdeen's city centre, Esslemont & Macintosh, known to all as E&M's, was considered rather high class back in 1963 when this picture was taken.

Long queues formed to see Aberdeen's first skyscraper flats at Ashgrove. This picture, taken by *Evening Express* and *Press and Journal* photographer Charlie Flett in March 1961, records a proud moment in the city's history.

'Noo dinna panic – if that's oil ye've struck – ye've pit Aiberdeen on its feet.' This wonderful cartoon by the late, great Jimmy Allan, is the only one of two I know of in existence, outwith his own family's collection. Jimmy's genius was not just in his ability to pen delightful cartoon figures, but to put the local news into comic context, mainly though his superb draughtsmanship. We took his cartoons for granted in the Fifties and Sixties, but it was only after he'd gone we realised there would never be another like him. This superb depiction of the cobbles coming up in Union Terrace, combined with the advent of North Sea oil, at the end of the Sixties, speaks volumes about the enormous changes the city was undergoing at the time.

A stunning aerial view of the newly constructed Aberdeen College of Commerce buildings in 1964, flanked by the Hardgate and, at the top of the picture, Holburn Street, with Nellfield Cemetery behind.

The end of an era for the *Evening Express* in November 1958, when the paper took on a brave new look, moving away from its traditional tabloid format to become a broadsheet. Here Lord Provost George Stephen, left, and Aberdeen Journals general manager John Noble, and specially invited guests, examine the first editions from the first run of the reborn *Evening Express*.

School and Student Days

Christmas 1967 and Lord Provost Robert Lennox receives a surprise Christmas card from the pupils of Ashgrove School. The delighted civic head is pictured here visiting the school to say a personal thank you and wish the children a Merry Christmas.

Young Air Training Corps cadets from 107 Squadron enjoy a day's flying in RAF Chipmunk trainer aircraft at Dyce in the early Sixties. In the pilot's seat is author David Smith.

Templars Park at Maryculter, second home to generations of Aberdeen Scouts, celebrated its 25th anniversary in 1961. Here scouts from all over the city enjoy a camp fire evening with their leaders.

Giving our photographer a cheery wave in May 1963 are members of the 27th troop (Hilton Church) Boy Scouts in Aberdeen to show what a great time they are having at their Templars Park camping ground in Maryculter.

Having a barrowload of fun at Templars Park is Ivor Hart as he wheels in more wood for the campfire in May 1963.

These smiling faces belong to boys from Robert Gordon's College who were making history in July 1958. The 30 lads were the first pupils to visit the German town of Regensburg after the cities twinned. Pictured at Joint Station before their departure the boys travelled by train and Channel ferry for the three-week visit. The party was led by Mr Robert Gill, who later became Rector of Aberdeen Grammar School. The other teachers on the trip were Neil Johnston and Robert Mowatt.

The statue of Aberdeen Grammar School's most famous old boy, Lord Byron, looks down on boys enjoying the snowy conditions in the playground in December 1969.

Costing £52,000, Aberdeen Grammar School swimming pool opened in October 1963 complete with three diving platforms and a springboard which clearly proved popular with these boys.

Top pupils of 1968 at Robert Gordon's College in Aberdeen were Peter Snape, left, with the Mackenzie Shield, and Alex Repper winner of the Otaki Shield. The Otaki scholarship, which includes a trip to New Zealand, commemorates the winning of a posthumous VC to former pupil Lieutenant Bissett Smith who was killed in action in World War One when his armed merchantman, *Otaki*, tackled a German raider, the *Moewe*, in the Pacific. After a 20-minute duel, with the *Otaki* sinking, he ordered the boats to be lowered to allow the crew to be rescued, but refused to desert his command and went down with his ship after inflicting considerable damage to the German and starting a fire which lasted three days. The winner of the shield is the guest of the New Zealand Shipping Company which owned the *Otaki* and the New Zealand government.

Andy Stewart and a group of Aberdeen schoolchildren record a night of Scottish songs for a television broadcast in November 1968.

A few old tyres and some home made play equipment was all it took for these kids to have great fun at Aberdeen's Gerrard Street adventure playground in 1969.

Now that's what you call a chute! These lucky bairns are having a fantastic time on the new chute provided for them at Heathryfold in 1969. And the innovative tree trunk stairway is almost a much fun as the slide.

Some swift consultation with the play leader seems in order as this farmer picks a wife during a party at Northfield Community Centre in October 1966. The little girl on the teacher's right is all set to step forward but her chum on the left seems to have something to say on the matter.

North-East child actors Jon Whiteley and Vincent Winter became overnight stars after appearing in the hit feature film *The Kidnappers* with Duncan Macrae in 1954. Torry loon Vincent aged five played the younger child Davy and John Whiteley of Monymusk aged six, played his brother Harry in the film about a Scots family in Nova Scotia. The boys wowed audiences all over the world and received honorary Oscars. Vincent was spotted by a talent scout while a pupil at Walker Road School. He died aged 50 in 1998.

After receiving an honorary Oscar for his role in *The Kidnappers*, Monymusk schoolmaster's son Jon Whiteley went on to take further acting honours when he appeared with Dirk Bogarde in the feature film, *The Spanish Gardener*. Jon was discovered after taking part in a *Children's Hour* radio broadcast with his school.

Muriel Robson of Newburgh is a study in concentration as she wins the senior section of the hula hoop competition on the stage of the Regal Cinema in November 1958.

In a spin in 1958 is Christine Beattie of Seaton Road, Aberdeen. The eight-year-old makes hula-hooping look easy spinning no fewer than 12 hoops at one time.

On parade in 1951 are the young athletes from Ashley Road School who had the honour of leading the parade round the track in front of a large crowd at Linksfield Stadium.

Aberdeen Academy Dramatic Society in a scene from *The Dumb Wife of Cheapside* in the school hall in June 1961. Taking part (left to right) are David Smith, Stephen Alcock, Ewan McKerrell, Margaret Mackay and Sandra Gray.

Two of Aberdeen's top head teachers hear about careers in the Royal Air Force from the man at the top. Air Commodore G.M. McMinn chats with Mr John Skinner, rector of Aberdeen Grammar School, and Mr Alexander Goldie, rector of Aberdeen Academy, on a visit to the RAF recruiting office in September 1969.

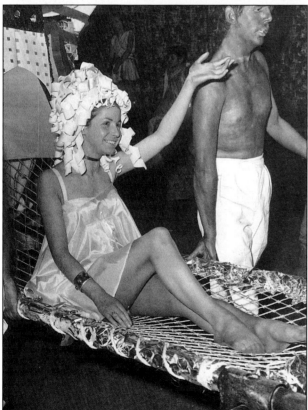

Looking gorgeous in her Baby Dolls is 19-year-old Arts Queen, Carole Moulsdale as she makes a spectacular entrance at the 1969 Aberdeen University Arts Ball held at the Beach Ballroom.

Sitting pretty are 1968's Aberdeen Students Charities Queen Wendy Corbett and her attendants. Eighteen-year-old Wendy of Summerhill Drive, Aberdeen, was in her second year as a pharmacy student at Robert Gordon's Institute of Technology. Flanking her are (right) Jennifer Brunnen, 18, of Gladstone Place, Aberdeen, a first-year physiotherapy student at Woolmanhill, and (left) 20-year-old Retna Ayadurai, from Malaysia, a first year student at the School of Domestic Science.

Silence please! These busy students, like generations before them, hit the books at Aberdeen Public Library's reference department in March 1966. A hive of research, during the course of that year alone 110,000 consultations were made helping countless students get their degrees.

Headphones on, these students concentrate hard on separating the dots from the dashes as Principal C. Mulvey takes a class on Morse Code at Aberdeen Wireless College in July 1961.

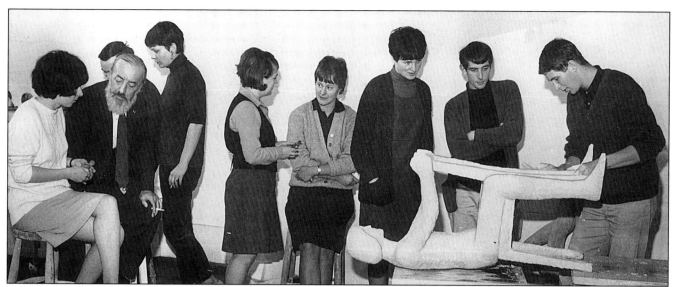

Former Aberdeen Lifeboat coxwain Leo Clegg with fourth-year sculpture students in the new sculpture work room when it opened at Gray's School of Art in 1966.

It was about 50 years ago that the great red toga debate raged among students at Aberdeen University. In our picture students are marching an effigy through Aberdeen streets to be 'hanged' at Marischal College. This 'funeral' parade was part of a campaign to re-introduce the university's ancient red togas. The tradition of wearing a gown had been in decline for more that 40 years. However, the cost of the togas was considered too high for students at £10.00 so the University Court subsidised them so they could be bought for £3 3s (£3.15). The traditionalists won a two-day vote on the matter with 500 students backing the return of the togas. In fact the university calendar had stated for as long as people could remember that 'all students are expected to wear the scarlet gown and trencher'. But even that could not eventually save the toga from the march of time.

Farsyerdojo was the slogan for Aberdeen Students Charities Campaign in 1968. Not much doubt where the 'do' ended up that year – in the collecting cans of hundreds of students. Here at the National Commercial Bank at the corner of Union Street and St Nicholas Street the pennies are totted up by hand in the traditional way. Not even those scattered across the floor were missed.

There's no getting away for this lad as a determined witch swoops down on him on her broomstick to put a spell on his pennies during the 1962 Aberdeen Students Charities Campaign.

No outfit was too ridiculous for Aberdeen University students in their annual charities campaign. And the bowler hatted gent complete with brolly and spats was no exception as he paraded the streets liberating the crowds from their cash in 1962.

No names survived this 1962 picture taken on the steps of Aberdeen Music Hall, but Pocahontas and Jenny Wren certainly made their mark on that year's students campaign.

This wee lad seems less than impressed with the two big heads who are after his cash. Aberdeen Students Charities Campaign reaches its climax for 1967 with the annual Saturday street collection on Saturday, April 20. Our picture shows medical student David Garioch of Milltimber and girlfriend Chris Shaw, who was studying science, having no problem extracting the pennies form these excited youngsters.

The 1966 Aberdeen Charities Campaign students show. One Degree Over, was a monster success thanks to a great cast including students Judy Gibb and Joan Hall. The girls are seen here perched on the beast which led the Torcher procession.

Trad Jazz was all the rage in the Swinging Sixties and this band helped to swing loadsacash out of the crowds during the Aberdeen Students Charities Campaign Torcher procession of 1965.

Naturalist and broadcaster Peter Scott gets behind the bar for Aberdeen University students. The son of famous explorer, Scott of the Antarctic, Peter was celebrating his victory in the 1961 rectorial campaign with his supporters in the Kirkgate Bar. He is seen here examining the inscription on the tankard with which he was presented.

Radio comedian, Professor Jimmy Edwards, star of the popular *Take it From Here* series, celebrates with a pint after winning the Aberdeen University rectorial election in 1952.

Baby it's cold outside – but nobody's feeling the chill on November 1966 as supporters of Sir Dugald Baird in the Aberdeen University rectorial campaign line up for the start of the pram race down Union Street. Winners were 'baby' Janet Ellis and 'mummy' Jerry O'Regan, both Arts students.

Students do a spot of busking outside the Gaumount Cinema in 1968 in a bid to fill their collecting cans. ABOBLEDOO was that year's slogan and a bob or two was certainly raised.

Five fabulous girls in one fabulous car. Aberdeen Students Charities Queen Louise Giles (centre) is flanked by attendants (left to right) Rosemary Jones, Anne Barnett, Belina McLeod, and Elaine Osborne on board the MG competition car being run in conjunction with the film *Some Girls Do* showing at the Odeon in February 1968.

Bloodied but ecstatic, a student celebrates victory after the 1966 Aberdeen University rectorial battle at Marischal Quad.

The crowds turn out for the start of the 1962 Aberdeen Students Charities Campaign torcher procession. The parade, complete with monster and baby monster, makes its way from the quad at Marischal College towards Queens Cross before turning back into the city centre. In the front of the picture a student in a bobby's helmet and fake beard, brandishing a toy gun, risks all to try to shake a few bob out of a police sergeant.

Two students grapple among the debris while the battle goes on around them. The year is 1966, the place – Marischal College quadrangle. Aberdeen University's traditional rectorial battle is in full swing. Elected rector was Highland business tycoon Frank Thomson, succeeding Everest hero Sir John Hunt.

This 1961 picture shows the full cast in the opening scene of that year's students show, *Rage of Kings*, at His Majesty's Theatre during gala week.

The focus on Northern Ireland switched to Aberdeen in October 1969 when one of the province's most prominent politicians, Bernadette Devlin spoke in a major debate on the troubles. Almost 1,000 students and members of the public packed the Mitchell Hall to hear the Independent MP for Mid-Ulster take part in an Ulster Teach-In. Hundreds were turned away from the debate which also featured Eamon McCann from Derry Labour Party.

Thrice Miss Scotland, Susan Jones demonstrated she had brains as well as beauty when she graduated in maths from Aberdeen University in 1963. She is pictured here with her dad, world-famous wartime boffin, Professor R.V. Jones, after her graduation. One of the most beautiful women ever to grace that seat of learning, Susan took the Miss Scotland title three times in the Sixties. Born in Surrey in 1941 during a blitz attack by German bombers, Susan moved to Aberdeen with her family after the war when her dad became professor of natural philosophy at Aberdeen University. Her glittering public life started when she took a break from her studies to compete in the 1961 Miss Universe contest in Miami. After graduation she returned to the USA where she made her name as a model and television personality, before marrying her first husband, Dr John Parente. She turned down film offers to bring up her children, Gigina and John, before the couple divorced in the early Seventies. She later married Colonel Archie Addison when he was commanding officer at the Bridge of Don Barracks. She died in June 1992, aged 51 after a long battle against diabetes.

Middlefield Primary School choir pictured in 1952 on the steps of the Music Hall after winning the best choir in the Aberdeen Primary Schools Festival competition. Their teacher, Miss Isobel Strachan, is on the left.

The dreaded 11-plus over and Class 15 at Ashley Road School celebrated double success with a bus run to Royal Deeside in 1951. A creditable 28 out of 31 pupils were destined for senior secondary schools. They are pictured here celebrating at their end of term party.

Thanks to the blackboard in the infant class at St Leonard's, Banchory Academy, we know that Wednesday, February 9, 1962, was not the sunniest of days – though there was never a dull moment in the classroom.

The third year girls choir at Banchory Academy practice for the upcoming Banchory and District Schools Music Festival in March 1962.

Immaculate in their whites, the 2nd X1 cricket team at Robert Gordon's College in 1955, though look closely and you'll notice there are only 10 in the line-up thanks to one of the team going sick on the day the photographer turned up. Back row, left to right: Charles Tennant, Tommy Steele, Murray Mowat, unknown, and Ron Fiddes. Front row: Keith Taylor, Dickson Cormack, Charles Simpson, Richard Walker and Derek Gray.

Coronation Year and in the summer of 1953 the 15th/28th Boys' Brigade were camped at Carrbridge, near Inverness. This picture brings back fond memories of the only holiday most of the boys would have that year. Our picture shows the great cameraderie of the BB in those days with Dougie Banks, George Fraser, Gordon Murray and Sandy Barber posing for the photographer before breakfast.

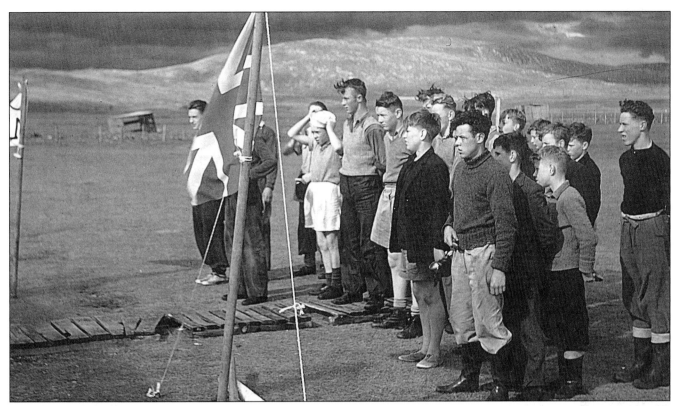

Boys of the 15th/28th Boys' Brigade line up outside the big marquee waiting to go in for breakfast. The overcast sky and wellies tell their own story about the weather that summer.

Nine-year-old Alice Henry, assisted by the Revd James W. Tyrell, plants one of six rose bushes in the grounds of Mastrick Parish Church to mark the 50th anniversary of the Brownie movement, originally known as the Rosebuds. Girls from the church's packs – the 32nd A, B, C, D and E – took part in the ceremony in April 1964.

Curtain Up

Steptoe Junior says 'hello' to 18-month-old Yvonne Aitken, 43 Rosemount Viaduct, Aberdeen outside His Majesty's Theatre. Harry H. Corbett of *Steptoe and Son* fame was appearing in the play *Little Jock*. Also in the picture is Grandma Aitken.

Captain Hook, alias actor Ron Moody, points out the sights of Aberdeen to Peter Pan (Julia Lockwood) in Union Terrace Gardens in 1967. Julia was the only actress in theatre history to play Wendy twice and Peter four times in the J.M. Barrie play. In 1958 she appeared at His Majesty's Theatre as Wendy in *Peter Pan* with her mother, screen star Margaret Lockwood.

In 1960, two years after screen star Margaret Lockwood appeared as Peter Pan at His Majesty's Theatre, daughter Julia takes over the role for the first time.

A backstage worker gets scenery ready for a forthcoming production at HM Theatre in 1969.

A cleaner makes sure everything is ship-shape for the next show at HM Theatre in February 1969.

In March 1965 the *Evening Express* featured this superb picture of the entire cast of *The Gondoliers* on the stage of the Art Centre. The Aberdeen Opera Company production ran for a week.

Manager James Donald, to the left of the open doors, turns disappointed fans away from HM Theatre after the *Andy Stewart Show* was cancelled in September 1964. Reluctantly, the singer had to admit the show could not go on after contracting laryngitis.

These three cheeky chappies turned heads in Schoolhill in September 1960. The hat-trick trio were left to right Jack Milroy, Alistair McHarg and Rikki Fulton who were starring in the *Five Past Eight Show* at His Majesty's Theatre. Jack and Rikki later teamed up to create Scotland's favourite comedy duo, Francie and Josie.

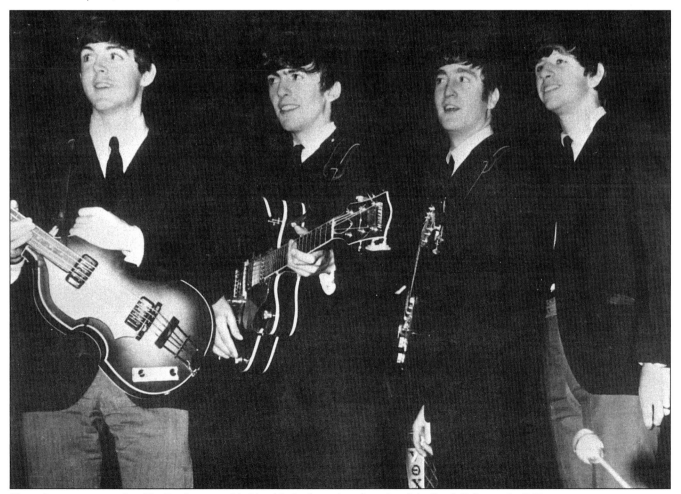

Not quite megastars yet but The Beatles were a big hit with the fans when they played the Beach Ballroom in 1963.

The Sharp suits, the pencil ties and the Buddy Holly specs mean it's Freddie and the Dreamers, putting everything into their fun act at the Capitol in May 1964.

A section of the sell-out crowd which had a great night of rock 'n' roll with Freddie and the Dreamers at the Capitol in May 1964. Note the girl in the centre of the picture, about four rows from the front, wearing her rollers under a headscarf. Look hard enough and you'll spot she's not the only one.

The famous quiff, the toothy grin, and who else could it be but Tommy Steele. Back in 1958 when the blond bombshell played the Capitol, he literally mesmerised the girls. The *Evening Express* had invited the amateur hypnotist to its teenage party in the Caledonian Hotel for 'the most sensational experiment ever conducted in Aberdeen.' The singer, who had been practising hypnotism since he was a boy, put 12 youngsters to sleep. He made some put their hands above their heads only to find they couldn't lower them, and he hypnotised *Evening Express* reporter John Lodge into hating the taste of cigarettes. Our picture shows the chart-topping star enjoying a round of applause after the party.

Tommy Steele has one of his fans eating out of his hand following his sell-out rock 'n' roll spectacular at The Capitol in July 1958.

Well-known Aberdeen councillor Frank Magee's daughter, Carolyn, and fiancé Stuart Begg, get the VIP treatment from Andy Stewart and band leader Ian Powrie, after turning up at His Majesty's Theatre to discover they were the 100,000th visitors to the show in September 1966.

Aberdeen cinema foreman James McGregor makes Andy Stewart's eyes pop as he receives his Fix-the-Ball cheque for £575 in February 1960. Noticing James' plastered left wrist, Andy cracked: 'You'll break the other counting the money.'

Andy Stewart goes on his knees to plead for a slice of the £2,700 Green Final Fix-the–Ball cheque won by Mrs Mary Gilchrist. Mary was invited on to the stage at HM Theatre in July 1966 to receive her cheque during Andy's show.

The Palace Cinema off Bridge Street in 1959 just before it closed to become a dance hall.

The News Cinema in Diamond Street was given a whole new look as well as a new name in 1959. Reborn as the Curzon, specialising in continental films, patrons could still hear the strains of the band next door in the Palais Ballroom during the film presentations. The first film shown in the Curzon was *Around the World With Nothing On.*

Rock 'n' roll is here to stay in Aberdeen in January 1957. Fans of the new sound didn't mind getting soaked as they queued in the rain outside The Capitol in Union Street to see Bill Haley and the Comets in *Rock Around the Clock*.

Aberdeen has never seen anything like it before – or since. When Alfred Hitchcock's thriller *Psycho* opened at the Caumont Cinema in Union Street in October 1960. The queues snaked all the way from the cinema opposite Diamond Street, along Crown Street, down Windmill Brae and up the other side. Police were out in force to monitor the queues for several nights.

Actor Richard Todd was mobbed by fans when he performed the official opening of Britain's most up-to-date cinema, the Regal in Aberdeen's Shiprow in July 1954. It was only with police assistance he was able to break clear of the crowd, which had waited for an hour in pouring rain to greet him. The Shiprow was the setting for the Gaiety, Aberdeen's first permanent picture house which introduced talking pictures to the city almost 50 years earlier. Here, the Regal is pictured in 1961, showing *Saturday Night and Sunday Morning*.

A touch of New Mexico in the heart of Aberdeen – that was the Spanish-style Casino Cinema at the top of the Beach Boulevard. It showed films which had previously featured in front rank cinemas like the Odeon or Regal.

Comedian Johnny Victory travelled in style when he brought his show to the Tivoli in June 1962. Here Johnny shows off his magnificent vintage Rolls-Royce parked at the rear of the Station Hotel.

Accordionist Will Starr takes centre stage with Calum Kennedy as the stars of the final show at the Tivoli join hands in September 1963 for a poignant rendition of *Auld Lang Syne*. Far right in the picture are the Alexander Brothers next to Sally and Joe Logan.

Great Sports

One of the greatest names in women's tennis and badminton in Scotland in the Sixties and Seventies, Helen Kelly of Aberdeen, in action at the Duthie Park in 1967.

Helen Kelly's brother, George, played for the Dons in the Fifties before becoming a top-class Scottish international tennis ace. George, who took a host of titles during his career, died aged 65 in Aberdeen Royal Infirmary. George is pictured (right of the picture) in 1956 after beating T. Wood to win the North-East of Scotland Singles Championship at the Four Courts Tournament.

A clear eye and a steady aim – these marksmen were on target at the 1963 Wapinshaw at Black Dog, near Bridge of Don. Drawing a bead at the city's top shooting event, are, left to right, A. Ewen, Kemnay, G. Taylor, Mintlaw, and J. Daniel of Strichen.

Aberdonian Athole Still, a member of the 1952 British Olympic swimming squad at Helsinki, was one of Andy Robb's swimming 'babes' while a pupil at Robert Gordon's College. He later made a name for himself as an opera singer and sports agent.

Table tennis ace Richard Yule in action in 1969. The Aberdonian in his time won more Scottish caps than any other sportsman. He represented Scotland on 270 occasions and won the Scottish championship eight times.

November 1966 and four years after retiring from the international swimming scene, Ian Black took the plunge again when he married Miss Alison Walker, of Menzies Road, Aberdeen, at King's College Chapel. They met when Ian was coaching young swimmers and she went on to win the Scottish junior breaststroke title.

Aberdeen's Olympic swimming star, Ian Black, shocked the city when he announced his retirement in June 1962 on the eve of his 21st birthday. It was the end of a golden career in which he won it all – except Olympic success. Seven years at the top brought him every honour including gold medals in the Empire Games, three golds in the European Games, two world records and numerous European, Empire, British and Scottish records. His failure to get a medal in the final of the 400 metres freestyle at the Rome Olympics in 1960 proved a major blow. The decision was surrounded by controversy. Ian thought he had touched third and so did millions of TV viewers. But the decision went to John Konrads on the strength of an unofficial electronic device after the decision of the umpires was equally divided. The greatest swimmer Aberdeen ever produced, Ian, in December 1958, was voted BBC Sportsview Personality of the year. Moments after receiving the trophy at the ceremony in the Grosvenor House Hotel, London, he was named *Daily Express* Sportsman of the Year. Ian is pictured holding both trophies after the presentation.

A brave three-year experiment to attract bigger attendances to Aberdeenshire Cricket Club was undertaken in 1957 with the signing of top West Indian batsman Rohan Kanhai as professional. That the experiment failed was in no way due to the brilliant batsman who in his first two seasons scored over 1150 runs in championship matches alone.

One of Aberdeenshire Cricket Club's greatest servants, Dr George Youngson, earned 25 caps for his country in a 17-year career. 'Big George' served the county from 1946 until 1962, being converted from an opening batsman with Gordonians in the Strathmore Union to an opening bowler. The 6ft 5in pace man was Aberdeenshire's only representative in the Scotland side which faced Don Bradman's mighty Australians at Mannofield in the 'Don's' farewell appearance on British soil in 1948. He died aged 62 in Aberdeen in 1982.

One of the greatest rugby players Aberdeen ever produced, international Ian McRae of the Gordonians club makes a dramatic pass during a match in 1969. The fiercely competitive scrum-half played six times for Scotland between 1967 and 1972.

The young lad on the left of our picture can't wait to start kicking a ball about as Col. E. Birnie Reid officially opens the Lads' Club superb new pavilion at Woodside on the night of May 18, 1967.

Still turning out for Aberdeen Wanderers in his 40s, Ronnie 'Bomber' Comber played rugby for Aberdeen Grammar FPs for 30 years. The former Scottish international reserve, paid a high price in the form of three broken collar bones, broken fingers, ankles, breast bone, ribs and sundry bruises and gashes. His nickname came from his habit of putting his head down and running straight at the opposition and diving over other players ready to touch down.

In-out, in-out – and it's in and out between the trawlers at Aberdeen Harbour for these competitors in the Inter Club Regatta on the River Dee in February 1965. Our picture shows the Aberdeen Academy 1st crew on the nearside taking on the Aberdeen University 1st crew at Point Law.

One of Aberdeen's best known bookies since the Thirties, Bobby Morrison, who owned a chain of 10 betting shops in Aberdeen, until selling out to William Hill. Bobby was also a director of Aberdeen Football Club. He is pictured here in the late Eighties.

Aberdeen's bookies were household names in the Fifties and Sixties with many of them standing at the dogs – making a book at Aberdeen Greyhound Stadium at Bridge of Dee – since before World War Two. Among them was my dad, Bill Smith, who opened his own office in Rosemount Place after learning his craft before World War Two as a turf commission agent with Andy Buchan in Belmont Street. With his brother Eric clerking he was a well-known figure at the dogs until the stadium closed to make way for a supermarket.

Aberdeen Sea Swimmers Club honour their secretary and treasurer, Andy Robb at his retirement dinner in the Dee Motel. Founder member Andy, who served the club for 42 years, received a watch from president Mr W. Oliver. A towering figure in the world of swimming, he spent 30 years on the staff of Robert Gordon's College, producing a succession of swimmers of international standard, most significantly Olympic swimmer Ian Black. Under his guidance Gordon's College teams won their school a reputation as one of the top swimming schools in Britain. Before joining the college, Andy, a lifelong member and former captain of the Dee Swimming Club, and a founder member of Aberdeen Sea Swimmers Club was with Aberdeen Corporation as beach rescue and instructor at the Beach Baths. He was twice awarded Royal Humane Society certificates for sea rescues.

Aberdeen Olympic swimming star Sheila Watt pictured modelling the official uniform of the Scottish team before flying off to represent her country in the Commonwealth and Empire Games in Perth, Western Australia. Sheila is wearing the team's trim dress and jacket in ice-blue terylene, with snappy flowerpot hat, white court shoes, gloves and shoulder bag.

The victorious Banks o' Dee team which won the North Regional Junior FA Championship in May 1969 by beating Burghead Thistle over two games. Back row (left to right): R. Plenderleith, R. Fraser, A. Irvine, A. Paterson, B. D'Arcy, K. Massie and R. Carrol. Front row: I. Fraser, W. Pirie, R. Morris, A. Keir and W. Falconer.

Lord Provost Robert Lennox boots the ball into the goalmouth at Heathryfold Park in June 1968 after officially opening the new Sunnybank FC Social Club. Members of the committee line up in goal with the Lady Provost.

The Banks o' Dee A team who retained the Aberdeen FC Trophy by beating King Street A by a convincing 5-0 in the final at Pittodrie in May 1967.

Heroes all… the Banks o' Dee team who took the Scottish Junior Cup home in 1957. Back (left to right): Ogston, McKenzie, Anderson, Lornie, Ewen, and Fraser. Front: Fowler, Studd, Walker, Robertson and Warrender.

Fleet-footed centre-forward Paddy Buckley, one of the Dons' greatest-ever players, takes on Rangers big George Young.

High Spirits… the Dons of 1967, and Wee Alickie, look forward to competing in the European Cup Winners Cup for the first time after losing 2-0 to Celtic in the Scottish Cup Final earlier the same year. Left to right: Jim Storrie, Tommy McMillan, Jimmy Wilson, Jens Petersen, Jinky Smith, Davie Johnson, who later walked our on senior football, Harry Melrose, Ally Shewan, Eddie Buchanan and Jim Whyte. After trouncing KR Reykjavik 14-1 on aggregate, the Dons lost out to Standard Liege in the next round despite winning 2-0 at Pittodrie through goals from Frank Munro and Harry Melrose. This was Jimmy Wilson's last game for the Dons – on December 8, 1967, he joined Motherwell in exchange for George Murray.

Magic of the cup. A packed Pittodrie in happy mood for the Scottish Cup third-round tie against Rangers in February 1962. A 2-2 draw ensued, with George Kinnell scoring from the penalty spot and Billy Little adding the second. Four days later, however, Rangers cruised home 5-1 in the replay at Ibrox Stadium. Bobby Cummings got Aberdeen's consolation goal.

Christmas Eve 1966… and Celtic supremo Jock Stein in pensive mood. A Harry Melrose goal earned the Dons a 1-1 draw. The return at Celtic P:
in April also resulted in a draw, this time goalless.

Aberdeen's Hughie Baird forces Hibs' goalie Lawrie Leslie to make this brilliant save during a Scottish League match at Pittodrie in October 1958. Aberdeen won 4-0 with Billy Little (second from right) grabbing a hat-trick and Archie Glen completing the tally with a penalty. Do you recognise the Hibs' star on the left? Yes it's none other than Eddie Turnbull, who went on to become the Aberdeen manager in 1965.

League Cup action from Pittodrie in August 1956. Celtic 'keeper Dick Beattie saves with Aberdeen's Graham Leggat – recently honoured by the Canadian FA – ready to pounce. Celtic legends Sean Fallon (left) and Bertie Peacock await developments. The score? 1-1 to Celtic, with Harry Yorston on target for the Dons.

Hard luck, brother! Aberdeen's Archie Glen (right) and his brother, Alec, of Queen's Park, leave the field content after captaining their respective sides at Pittodrie in a Scottish League match on September 15, 1956. Aberdeen won 2-1 with Jackie Hather and Paddy Buckley the marksmen for the Dons.

A classic picture of two of Aberdeen FC's all-time greats. Toothless George Hamilton gives 'golden boy' Harry Yorston, the Dons' star goal-getter of the Fifties, a hug after he scored a late equaliser in the Scottish Cup Final against Rangers in 1953. Unfortunately the Dons lost the replay. Sadly George died earlier this year.

The glory days come to Aberdeen in October 1955. Dons captain and right back Jimmy Mitchell is chaired to the waiting bus with the League Cup on the team's return to a fantastic welcome by one of the biggest crowds of fans the city had ever seen.

Glory Days

The team which took the Dons to double glory in 1955 was Martin, Mitchell, Smith, Allister, Young, Glen, Leggat, Yorston, Buckley, Wishart and Hather.

For thousands of Dons fans hitting their 60s and over, these are the original heroes of Pittodrie. Even Alex Ferguson – Gothenburg and all – would readily agree that a football first is truly something special. The magnificent feat of these Dons legends back in season 1954-55 has never been properly recognised – until now.

For the die-hards of that memorable era the names of the first-ever Dons team to clinch the Scottish League championship roll off the tongue as if it were yesterday. Those were the golden days of brilliant, attacking football with skills to be envied despite having to combat a heavy leather football which was more a lethal weapon in bad weather. The facts speak for themselves.

The Dons played 30 League matches on their way to creating history, scoring 73 goals and conceding only 26. The dashing and cavalier Paddy Buckley – the late Jock Stein once ripped off his shorts in sheer frustration – led the way with a tally of 17, including a hat-

trick against Rangers. Next came 'golden boy' Harry Yorston with 12, while 'jack-in-the-box' Graham Leggat banged in 11, Flying winger Jackie Hather bagged nine, with crafty inside-left Bobby Wishart adding eight. Imagine – and entire forward line scoring goals!

A tremendous run of nine games without defeat, emphasised by the fact that only 19 players were utilised in the entire season which consisted of 42 competitive matches (30 League, six League Cup and six Scottish Cup-ties). The inspirational Archie Glen and Englishman Jackie Hather boasted 100 per cent records with 42 appearances, ably backed by Alec (Sliding Tackle) Young with 41, Buckley (40), speedy right back and captain Jimmy Mitchell (40), goalkeeper Fred (Mr Dependable) Martin (39) and Leggat, Yorston and the versatile Billy Smith (all 36). Then came Iron Man, right-half Jackie Allister on 32 and Wishart on 29.

These 11 go down in soccer history for sheer entertainment, talent, breathtaking and daredevil football, teamwork at its finest, and, sadly lacking today, pure enjoyment. For the superb Glen, who died in 1998, his finest moment came when he scored the goal which

clinched Aberdeen's first-ever Scottish League Championship. The date was Saturday, April 19, 1955 and the venue Shawfield Park. Glen's penalty sealed a 1-0 victory over Clyde and sparked off more celebrations than Hogmanay.

By coincidence, Aberdeen also clashed with Clyde in the semi-final of the Scottish Cup the same season. The first game at Easter Road resulted in a 2-2 draw – a brace for Buckley – but it was Clyde who battled through 1-0 in the replay.

Wonderful days for a wonderful team – and in October further glory when the Dandy Dons lifted the Scottish League Cup, with Leggat worthily earning the plaudits. The Scotland international grabbed six goals in four matches in the knock-out stages including a hat-trick in the first leg against Hearts at Pittodrie.

To the delight of thousands of fans all over the North-East, Leggat and Wishart grabbed the goals which dumped Rangers 2-1 in the semi-final at Hampden Park. On to the final against St Mirren on October 22 and triumph, courtesy of a Jimmy Mallon own-goal and that man Leggat.

Happy days.

Pittodrie as it was in the 1950s. Known then as Pittodrie Park, the bunnetted fans on its terracings never dreamed that one day the Dons would play in the ultra-modern, all-seater stadium of today.

The Fifties represented a tremendous era for crack Aberdeen junior sides Sunnybank and Banks o' Dee. Sunnybank became the first city side to lift the Scottish Junior Cup in 1954 when they beat Lochee Harp 2-1 in the final at Hampden Park on Saturday, May 22 in front of 24,600 fans. The history makers were: Johnny Stephen, Eric Harper, Jimmy Murray, Bobby Simpson, Teddy Scott, Willie Garden, Willie Chalmers, Billy Yeoman, Dickie Cruickshank, Jimmy Ingram and Billy Stephen.

Celebration time for Sunnybank supporters at Aberdeen Joint Station the morning after its Scottish Junior Cup triumph in 1954.

The highly-successful Cove Rangers FC team of 1964-65 pictured here at Allan Park, Cove Bay, with the Aberdeen FC Cup, Bowie Cup, Barclay Cook Cup and the League Championship Shield – they were undefeated in the League. That season they went to 35 games undefeated and then lost their one and only match – to Aboyne in the semi-final of the North of Scotland Cup. Winning four trophies made it Cove's best season in the 20-year period after World War Two which included 10 League Championships and winning the Aberdeen FC Cup 12 times – all at Pittodrie. The players are: Back row (left to right): George Mavor, David Hird, Billy Napier, Jim Wood, Arthur Taylor, Tommy Steele and Robin Johnston. Front row: Sandy Coull, Jim Forbes, Ron Fiddes, Davie Stewart, Eddie Robertson, Pat Carrol and Billy Still. Ron remembers: 'The team talk in the dressing room before the game was brief and to the point. Jimmy Coull, the president, told us that Cove Rangers had never lost a final at Pittodrie, this would be Cove's 12th appearance in the final in 18 seasons and he did not expect us to lose that night. The upshot was we beat Mugiemoss three goals to one.'

They were the best the Boy's Brigade had to field in 1957. Here the Aberdeen Battalion Football Select pose for the photographer at BB Headquarters. Back row (left to right): D. Lamont (63rd); M. Davidson (14th); I. West (15th); H. Blair (63rd); D. Simpson (15th); and Frank Rae (63rd) trainer. Front row: W. McKenzie (37th); L. Donaldson (2nd); R. Fiddes (15th); D. Fulton (30th) and I. Digby (18th).

Scottish international Graham Leggat hands over the Macmillan Shield and Munro Cup to the 15th company, winners of the season 1956-57 at the Aberdeen Battalion presentation of prizes at BB Headquarters in Crimond Place. A year later Fulham paid Aberdeen FC £16,000 for Leggat.

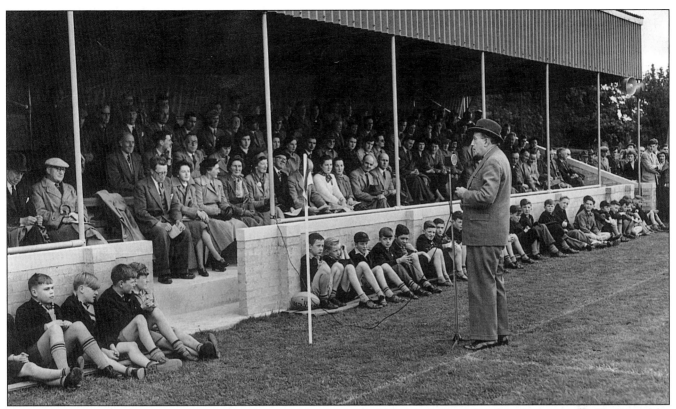

Boys sit along the front of the new stand at Robert Gordon's College's playing fields at Seafield in September 1954. Parents, staff and members of the former pupils' association listen as Baillie James Mackie accepts the new stand from the association on behalf of the governors.

Aberdeen boxing legend Johnny Kidd in action against Johnny McLaren in 1958. Kidd's career was littered with golden moments as an amateur and professional. He virtually monopolised the Scottish lightweight title from the late Fifties until the mid-Sixties and he came close to winning the British title and was one fight away from a crack at the world crown. His first professional title was won on his own doorstep at Linksfield Stadium in 1958 when 2,500 fans cheered him on to a knockout win over Johnny McLaren of Coatbridge for the Scottish Lightweight Championship.

Green Final Top Ten Champion... that was Sandy Pirie in 1969, then a leading amateur with the Hazlehead club. Two years earlier Sandy had the distinction of representing Great Britain and Ireland in the Walker Cup match against America who won 15-9 at Royal St George, Sandwich. Sandy also appeared for Great Britain Europe and played for Scotland between 1966 and 1975. He twice finished runner-up in the Scottish Amateur final. In our picture Sandy receives the Green Final Trophy from Bill Kerr, president of the North-East District, watched by Ivor Phillips, Ian Creswell, John Taylor, Hugh Adam, Brian Dignan and Denis Miller, who went on to become president of the Scottish Golf Union in season 1987-88.

In the groove... that's Harry Bannerman, pictured in action in 1968 little knowing that three years later he would be representing Great Britain in the Ryder Cup at St Louis, Missouri. Bannerman halved his first singles match against the legendary Arnold Palmer and then defeated Gardner Dickinson 2 and 1 in the afternoon. That was a tremendous performance, as, until then, Dickinson had never lost a Ryder Cup match. In the four-somes, Harry, playing out of Cruden Bay at that time, teamed up with Bernard Gallacher to beat Billy Casper and Miller Barber 2 and 1. He was then paired with Peter Townsend, and went down 2 and 1 to Jack Nicklaus and Gene Littler and then by only one hole to Palmer and Nicklaus.

Car enthusiasts enjoy the summer sun at the Fintry Hill Climb in July 1969.

When Aberdeen Indoor Bowling Rink opened in October 1963, Norman Allan, President of the Scottish Bowling Association (Indoor) described it as the finest not only in Scotland, but the whole of Britain. The stadium in Summerhill Road, had the largest roof-span in the country – 150ft. The club opened with 1100 members – the target figure. With 400 women members and a large waiting list, the club was assured of success. In December the following year, the club reported a 19-month trading profit of £10,307 and a 6 per cent dividend was paid out to members.

Aberdeen Greyhound Racing Stadium at Bridge of Dee, pictured in August 1968, a year before it closed to make way for a superstore. On the opposite side of Garthdee Road can be seen the recently built Dee Motel.

They're off! The first race ever staged at the Bridge of Dee dog racing track on June 7, 1933. The winner of the four-runner scratch event was 1-2 favourite Rimutaka (trap 1). The Sixties saw the track's closure, on October 4, 1969 to be exact.

Protest and Conflict

Big Jim Taylor, New York-based leader of the Close Brethren religious sect on a visit to Aberdeen in 1964 when he broke his silence and spoke to reporters during a rally at the Music Hall. Dubbed the Archangel by the Scottish media, he presided over a worldwide split in the ranks of the Brethern when he claimed he had been falsely accused of adultery during a visit to Aberdeen and that he had been held against his will in a room in a city house. In 1965 a Peterhead vet refused to put down any more pets belonging to members of the strict sect after it was alleged Big Jim had issued an edict: 'Save all your love for your religion.' The vet said: 'All sorts of excuses were given why their pets had to die. Some admitted they were Close Brethern, others wouldn't.'

Powis Crescent is transformed by an ugly mound of rubbish during the dustcart drivers' strike in December 1969.

Two little girls get rid of their family's rubbish by wheeling it to the tip at Dancing Cairns quarry on a baby's pushchair during the dustcart drivers' strike in December 1969. A contractor's lorry and bulldozer clear rubbish, dumped by people at the side of the road leading to the quarry.

The end of 1969 was marked by a seven-week long council dustcart drivers' strike over pay in Aberdeen. With no refuse collections, rubbish piled high at unofficial dumps all over the city, and enterprising youngsters offered to take people's rubbish to council tips for cash. Unfortunately much of it ended up on unofficial dumps. At the end of the dispute, treasurer James Lamond said the strike achieved nothing that could not have been resolved by negotiation. Aberdeen Corporation Cleansing Department staff listen to speakers during a strike meeting at their Poynernook Road depot.

Two protestors deliver a Nazi salute to the government of South Africa from atop the goalposts at the Springboks match against North and Midlands at Linksfield Stadium in 1969 as bemused bobbies look on.

In 1969 surprise tactics floored anti-apartheid demonstrators at the South African rugby team's match against a North/Midlands side at Aberdeen's Linksfield Stadium. A team of police officers, stripped to shirts and running shoes, sprinted on to the pitch following the fans' invasion and quickly despatched them from the ground. The bobby with his hands full in the front of our picture was on the fast track in more ways than one. PC David Beattie later became assistant chief constable of the Grampian force.

Anti-apartheid demonstrators crowd the police barrier at Linksfield Road in protest at the South African Rugby Team's appearance at Linksfield Stadium in Aberdeen in 1969.

Aberdeen busmen protest against pay and conditions outside the Town House in October 1967.

SNP councillor Alex McDonald walks past demonstrators into the Town House for a vital meeting on rent increases in the late 1960s. In the centre of our picture is Mrs Margaret Rose, a leading member of the city's Communist Party, who organised the demonstration.

A typical clash in the Town House in 1967. On his feet is Councillor Henry Hatch, hotly protesting the selection of Robert Lennox as Lord Provost. Councillor Bob Hughes, a future distinguished Labour MP for North Aberdeen, and tireless anti-apartheid campaigner, stands to support the selection.

Rail strikers march along Union Street in October 1962 to their protest rally against the Beeching Axe at the Market Stance in the Castlegate.

The unmistakable figure of the bow-tied Hector Hughes MP leads a procession of protestors at the 1960 May Day rally in Aberdeen. Ban the Bomb supporters and anti-apartheid protestors are prominent among the marchers as they emerge from King Street at the Castlegate and head for their rally in the Music Hall. Councillor Robert Lennox, a future Lord Provost, is just behind the fur-coated woman's Boycott South African Goods sign.

Not exactly a big turn-out on a rainy day to support the protestors taking part in the 1960 May Day rally in Aberdeen. But a pair of boys take more than a passing interest in the Ban the Bomb banners as the march heads up Union Street to hear the rousing speeches in the Music Hall.

Aberdeen Youth for Peace group protest over the Vietnam War near the Remembrance Day service at Schoolhill in November 1967.

As far back as 1960, Aberdeen University students were demonstrating against apartheid in South Africa and appealing to shoppers to boycott South African goods.

Police and Crime

Henry John Burnett, the last man to hang in Scotland and the first in Aberdeen, for 106 years. The fair-haired 21-year-old walked to the gallows where a hood was placed over his head and at one minute past eight on the morning of August 15, 1963, he paid the ultimate price for murder. Outside Craiginches Prison a silent crowd of more than 200 people stood vigil. There were no scenes. The only demonstrator was ice-cream salesman John Gibson who wore placards calling for the abolition of hanging. It had taken the jury just 25 minutes to find Burnett, of Powis Crescent, guilty of assaulting his lover, Margaret Guyan and of murdering her 27-year-old husband, merchant seaman Thomas Guyan by shooting him in the head with a shotgun in a house in Jackson Terrace. He was also found guilty of assaulting John Irvine of Canal Street, by presenting a loaded shotgun at him, threatening to shoot him and robbing him of his car. The murdered man's mother, Mrs Jeannie Guyan later said: 'I can find it in my heart to forgive Henry Burnett.' She told *Evening Express* reporters Ted Strachan and David King: 'If you see Mrs Burnett, give her my sympathy.'

Thirteen years after Tommy Guyan's murder, his wife, Margaret, who had been his killer's lover, revealed in a national newspaper that she had become an alcoholic and was living as a down and out in Aberdeen. She claimed the event had sent her spiralling into a world of alcohol binges and on to a drunken haze of wine drinking.

The Revd John Dickson, minister of St Fittick's Church, Torry, from 1957 to 1987 was one of the last people to speak to Burnett just before he was hanged. In his first in-depth interview about the hanging since that tragic day, Mr Dickson, now 81, told me of Burnett's remorse and how he firmly believes the condemned man found his faith through prayer in the days leading up to his execution. The softly-spoken former Craiginches prison chaplain spoke of the 21-year-old's calmness in the face of death and how he believes Burnett never meant to kill Guyan, merely to scare him with the shotgun. 'He was very sorry about it,' said Mr Dickson, 'he was bewildered. The way he spoke to me I don't think it was supposed to happen.' Mr Dickson, who visited Burnett every day for weeks before he went to the scaffold, recalled how they played cards and dominoes in the condemned cell, and of their conversations on many topics, including religion. 'He was marvellous,' said Mr Dickson. 'He spoke about everything, about his family, and about what happened. He convinced me that he acted on impulse. And I tried to impress on him that he was going to a better place.' Casting his mind back to the fateful morning of August 15, Mr Dickson said: 'I went through with him to the chamber where the execution was to take place and had a few words with him. I was holding the silver Cross of St John I had got on a visit to Iona. I held it up and I suppose it was the last thing he saw before the hood went on.' Immediately after the hanging, Mr Dickson said, everyone who had witnessed it was stunned. 'I felt terrible about it,' said Mr Dickson. 'I still feel it after all these years.' Mr Dickson later performed Burnett's funeral service.

A woman sheds a tear as she maintains a vigil outside Craiginches Prison in Aberdeen on August 15, 1963, minutes before the last execution in Scotland was carried out.

Two policemen on guard outside Craiginches Prison on August 15, 1963 on the morning of the execution of Henry Burnett for the murder of Tommy Guyan, while placard-bearing protestor John Gibson (29) demands the abolition of hanging. Burnett met his fate at one minute past 8am. Mr Gibson, of Stewart Terrace, paraded up and down the pavement wearing placards saying Abolish Legal Murder, and Vengeance is Mine Sayeth the Lord.

One of Aberdeen's most notorious killers, James Oliphant, is driven away from the High Court in Aberdeen after making an appearance in connection with the deaths of two children within 30 months of each other. Caithness-born Oliphant, 40, was given a life sentence in 1964 after he admitted two charges of culpable homicide and other indecent offences involving children. The High Court heard he had been certified as mentally defective in 1942 and original charges of murder were reduced on the grounds of diminished responsibility. His first victim was six-year-old June Cruickshank, killed near her Printfield Walk home while on an errand to a nearby shop in 1961. Seven-year-old George Forbes of Justice Street, died on an allotment at Castlehill in 1963. Both were found with their throats cut. The deaths sparked the biggest manhunt seen in Aberdeen, which lasted almost three years. Oliphant, who said he cut their throats because they screamed, died in Carstairs in March 1988.The High Court in Aberdeen was told the culpable homicide charges were infanto-sexual sadism, a form of perversion in which sexual gratification was gained by inflicting cruelty upon others. Driving the police car in the picture is detective Hamish Irvine, and sitting with Oliphant in the back is Bill Adams, who later became head of CID and subsequently deputy chief constable of Grampian Police.

The National Commercial Bank of Scotland at the junction of Union Street and Market Street, scene of a carefully-planned raid that went mysteriously wrong in August 1966. A gang from the south were believed to have been behind the attempt to rob one of the city's biggest branches. After getting into the rear of the building via the tunnel in East Green, the raiders removed stanchions in a back window which they had to reach with a 20ft ladder. A bungled attempt was made to burn open the strongroom door before the thieves fled empty-handed.

One of the great, unsolved murder mysteries in Aberdeen surrounded the death of Harry Bruce at his home in George Street in December 1964. The brother of Baillie Ronald Bruce, he was found dead with severe head injuries on the floor of his flat by his brother-in-law, Mr Charles Gillanders, who had called with newspapers and morning rolls. Despite extensive CID enquiries, thousands of people being interviewed in house to house enquiries, and appeals for information from the public through the *Evening Express* and *The Press and Journal*, no trace of his killer or killers was ever found. Police believed the motive for the killing was robbery.

On his way to serve 13 years in prison in January 1965 is killer James Connor Smith. He was sentenced to life by Lord Migdale for the 'motiveless murder' by stabbing of father-of-four James Millsom, 23, of Stewart Terrace on the body, leg and hand in Bill's Bar in Market Street. Smith, 22, found guilty after a three-day trial, did not go into the witness box and no defence evidence was led.

Max Garvie's lover, Trudy Birse and her husband, former policeman Alfred Birse, arrive to give evidence at the farmer's murder trial in Aberdeen in November 1968. He claimed Sheila Garvie had asked him for advice on how to clean fingerprints from a gun. Trudy later sold her story to a Sunday newspaper claiming she and Max had made love above the clouds in the cockpit of his two-seater plane.

Woman Police Sergeant Nessie Birse and WPC Frances Mutch escort Barbara Torliefson to the High Court in Aberdeen in March 1965 where she was jailed for seven years for the culpable homicide of Charles Brown at his flat in East North Street. Mr Brown drowned in his own blood from serious injuries to the floor of his mouth and throat. The jury's verdict indicated there had been a degree of provocation. Torliefson, who denied a charge of murder, had lodged a special plea of self-defence.

It was the North-East's murder trial of the century. The brutal slaying of wealthy Mearns farmer Max Garvie sparked one of the most sensational trials Scotland had ever seen. With its strong sexual elements of nudism, pornography, and affairs at the height of the Swinging Sixties, it attracted worldwide media attention, packing the public benches, and generating huge crowds outside the High Court in Aberdeen. Garvie's wife, Sheila and her lover Brian Tevendale, 22, were sentenced to life in 1969, after being found guilty of his murder. A second man, Alan Peters, who was in the house when Garvie died, walked free after the jury found the case against him not proven. Garvie, 34 at the time, protested her innocence, saying she was asleep beside Max when Tevendale woke her, hustled her into the bathroom, then made her watch the doorway of the bedroom where her children lay sleeping. She claimed she heard a muffled bang and saw the body being dragged downstairs in a groundsheet. Next day she steeled herself to clean the blood-spattered bedroom. Peters claimed he went to the house with Tevendale unaware of his intention to kill Garvie. He did as Tevendale told him because he had a gun and he feared for his life. He said Sheila had shown them into the house, given them drinks and showed them where to wait until Max was asleep. Tevendale claimed Garvie was shot by accident in a struggle with Sheila. Garvie had asked her to perform a sex act with the rifle, she refused, and in the struggle the gun went off. The witness who caused the greatest sensation was Trudy Birse, Tevendale's sister, and lover of Max Garvie. She gave lurid details of the sexual goings on and claimed Max had told her Sheila was frigid while she was prepared to carry out his unusual sexual demands. However, her most crucial evidence was that Tevendale told her he had killed Max in Sheila's presence after she had allowed him and Peters into the house and given them drinks. Trudy was the figure for whom the crowds reserved most hostility jeering and booing her and her husband. Alfred, a former police officer, in the street. When the angry mob pursued them down Union Street they took refuge in the *Daily Record* offices.

Handcuffed to PC Ian Wright, Allan Peters, who walked free after the trial, when the jury found the case against him not proven. He had lodged a defence of coercion by Brian Tevendale.

Brian Tevendale on his way to his trial for the murder of Max Garvie, in November 1968. He is handcuffed to Constable Warren Souden.

The farm at West Cairnbeg, Fordoun, where Max Garvie was murdered by his wife, Sheila and her lover Brian Tevendale, in May 1968, before his body was dumped in a culvert near St Cyrus.

Part of the angry crowd which pursued Trudy Birse and her husband, Alfred, down Union Street after her evidence at the Garvie murder trial in Aberdeen in December 1968. The couple sought refuge in the offices of the *Daily Record*, just yards from the court. Fred divorced her on the grounds of adultery in 1971. She later remarried but died in 1988 aged 50.

Max Garvie, brutally slain by his wife, Sheila and her lover Brian Tevendale, pictured with Sheila at a wedding in Montrose in 1965. She was released in September 1978 and published her autobiography, *Marriage to Murder, My Story*, in 1980. She re-married twice. Her third husband, Charlie Mitchell, died near their Stonehaven home in 1993.

Working Days

All together now – five students help the regular workers from the Links and Parks Department level and clear ground of stones and rubbish at Northfield to create playing fields for the community. Our picture, taken in August 1961, in the fast growing housing estate, shows John Breik, Alec Lawrie, Thomas Keith, Brian Anderson, A. Black, Alan Fowlie and Callum Campbell.

Keep off the Grass signs would have been a waste of time at Mastrick Shopping Centre in 1961. The grassed areas were so heavily used that grass seed had no chance to grow. So the finest turf was provided by Aberdeen Corporation's Links and Parks Department, whose men are pictured here doing an expert job in laying it.

Keen young lads get their heads down at the start of their careers with John M. Henderson and Co. Ltd, engineers, in Aberdeen. Pictured here is the first intake of apprentices for the firm's new training scheme which started in the first week of the new year in 1967.

Easy does it – and another giant load heads Down Under from Aberdeen in July 1965. This is the second of the two huge ball tube mills ordered from John M. Henderson and Co. Ltd by the Swanbank Power Station of the Southern Electricity Authority of Queensland, Australia. Weighing about 50 tons, around nine feet in diameter and 23ft long, the mills had to have a special cradle made for the trip. Each mill represented the heaviest load ever to leave the firm's works.

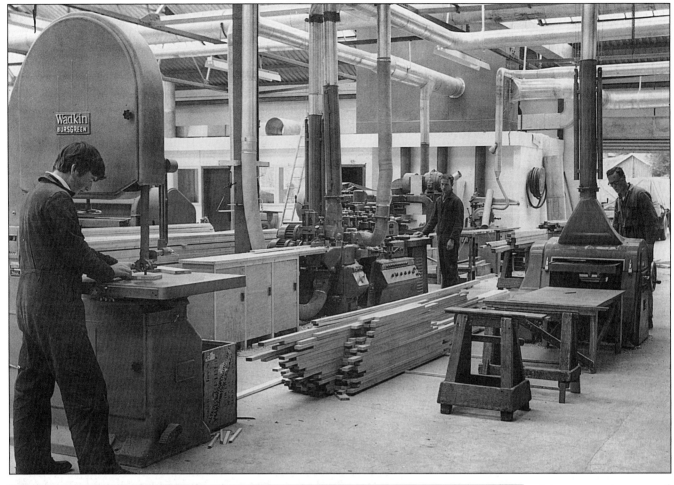

Joiners operate saw and planing machines at J. and A. Ogilvie's new factory at Albury Road in August 1968.

The scene after the flitting of one of Aberdeen's best-known family businesses, LISCO, from its Craigton Road premises, which it had occupied since 1935, to Mastrick's new industrial estate in 1967. Light Iron and Steel Construction Company Ltd, owned by the Hunter family, manufactured storage tanks, hoppers and silos, ducting and many other products in aluminium, steel and sheet metal. The company went into receivership in 1984.

LISCO apprentice Alan Heron looks happy in his work with another completed, galvanised bin at the firm's newly-opened premises at Mastrick Industrial Estate in 1967.

Four of the hand knitting machines in operation at Remploy's St Machar Road factory in November 1961. Hard at work are, left to right, John Redican, of Craigton Terrace, Alex Gillan of St Machar Drive, who joined the factory the week after it opened in 1951, T. Findlay, Seaton Place East, and Edward Nicol, of Moir Crescent, all Aberdeen.

Workers at one of Aberdeen's oldest granite works, James Wright and Sons (Aberdeen) Ltd, in their new 10,000-sq ft heated factory in September 1969, following a £70,000 modernisation project which the company hoped would lead to the revival of the granite industry. During building work on the site, occupied by the company since 1835, an old block of pink Peterhead granite was discovered bearing the inscription 'Please Shut the Well'. No trace of the well was ever found.

Two workers enjoy a chat in the training department at the new Ladybird factory at Tullos in February 1968. Seventeen machinists learned the manifold uses of the firm's modern sewing machines.

A hive of activity in Aberdeen University Press's new £100,000 premises in Farmers Hall Lane, Rosemount, when they opened in October 1963. The occasion was marked by the publication of an account of the firm from its foundation in 1840. Our picture shows the new machine room with ruling presses in the foreground.

No shame in being a butter fingers on this assembly line. These girls in their white headscarves make light work of tasty finger rolls at Strathdee's Northfield bakery in 1964.

Bon Bons by the yard at John E. Esslemont Ltd's new sweet factory. In 1968 the firm could scarce keep up with demand for its range of mouth-watering treats, Its egg and cream caramels were being consumed at the rate of 12,500 a day, its bon bons at a rate of 10,000,000 a year. And that was just a fraction of the firm's production.

A bird's-eye view of bakery workers hard at work in their whites at Strathdee's Northfield bakery in the week before Christmas and New Year, 1964. The Quarryhill Road factory cost almost £300,000 when it opened in 1956 and fulfilled a lifelong ambition for its owner, George Strathdee, who began business as a small baker in Union Grove in 1919. His grandad had a bakery where Aberdeen Central Library now stands in Schoolhill.

October 1965 was a red letter day for the Post Office in Aberdeen. Postmaster General Tony Benn, then known as Mr Anthony Wedgewood Benn, officially opened the modernised Crown Street building. He is seen here visiting the sorting office with Lord Provost Norman Hogg, Hector Hughes MP, and Aberdeen Postmaster Mr H.M. Morrow, who retired the following year after 45 years' service.

A busy scene at the head office of Aberdeen Post Office in Crown Street as the Christmas mail rush reaches its peak in December 1961.

Five-year-old Susan Jane McRae joins Lady Tweedsmuir, MP for South Aberdeen, in cutting the ribbon to mark the opening of Jamieson Brothers' new premises at Mastrick in April 1965. Susan's grandpa was managing director E.G. MacRae.

Everything goes modern at Joe Little's fish premises in Torry in 1968. Workers operate in bright, well-equipped conditions after a conveyor belt system was assembled in the filleting section.

These fish quines at Macfisheries factory in Poynernook Road, Aberdeen in June 1961 were stars of the fish processing industry. Filleters, skilled in wielding razor sharp knives, could turn fish into fillets at a blistering speed, working their way through vast quantities of fish during a shift.

Fish merchants' lorries and even an ice cream van form part of the queue in Poynernook Road as their drivers wait in hope for ice during the strike of workers at Aberdeen Ice Company in 1967.

Fishermen sort out a superb catch from the nets on the River Dee at Aberdeen in March 1963.

Not everyone was happy at the arrival on their doorstep of the new, innovative coal distribution yard in the heart of Kittybrewster in 1969. Residents kicked up a stour over the clouds of coal dust coming from the 10-acre site. Behind the giant piles of coal can be seen the homes of the complaining residents and Kittybrewster Primary School.

Coal was king in 1969 when the former British Railways goods yard at Kittybrewster, once a maize of rail tracks, made way for Ellis & Mchardy's new 10-acre coal yard with machinery, the first of its kind in Scotland capable of handling half-a-million tons a year. Bounded by Bedford Road and the main north rail line, the site was ideal for wagons unloading directly to the new conveyor belt system. The plant consisted of a boom stacker, a first in Scotland, which travelled on a 200-yards stretch of rail, fed from a conveyor belt carrying coal from the point where the rail wagons discharged.

Aberdeen Royal Infirmary had its own butchery department adjoining the main kitchen at Foresterhill. Meat would arrive in sides and the butcher's day was spent jointing it, as our 1955 picture depicts. Most would be cooked, prepared for the next day, fat rendered down, and bones turned to stock. He made potted head, produced more than 300 lbs of sausages a week, and vast quantities of the North-East's beloved mince. Hospitals had different ideas about healthy eating then and patients and staff were served meat no fewer than four times a week. Around 110 chickens a week were prepared, but mostly for patients on special diets. Fish was unpopular but around 740lbs a week was served to vary the menus and keep down budget costs.

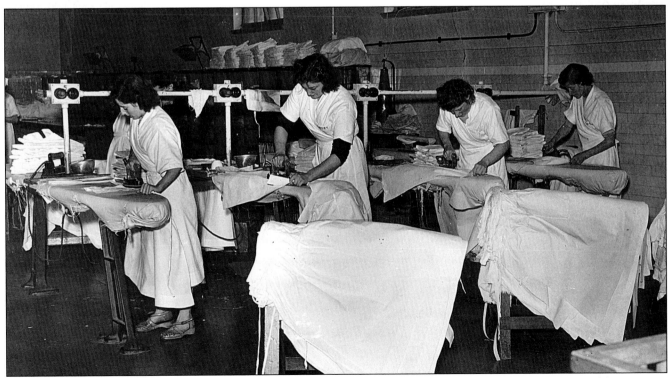

Dashing away with a smoothing iron these white-smocked workers at Aberdeen Royal Infirmary's Foresterhill laundry kept up a blistering pace in 1955. Some 53,000 articles a week were washed, many of them finished by hand. Nurses' dresses and aprons were pressed mechanically at top and tail before being finished by hand ironers. A special machine handled collars, cuffs, and belts, which were starched in an oak tub like a butter churn. This gave the nurses that crisp look which lasted all day.

Quarry manager John Ross and Mr Robert Murison measure an enormous block of granite at the bottom of Rubislaw Quarry in the heart of Aberdeen's West End in 1964. For around 200 years the quarry produced the famous glistening grey stone of which great public works around the world, like Sidney Harbour Bridge and London's Waterloo Bridge were made. The deepest man-made hole in Europe the quarry is 465ft deep, 900ft long and 750ft wide. It is a proud boast of the Granite City that 'half o' Aiberdeen came oot o' that hole.'

The derelict wooden steps which snake up from the bottom of Rubislaw Quarry were used by generations of workmen to get to and from their work.

Come the late Sixties when this picture was taken, Finzean Sawmill had been in the same family for generations. Here father and son, David Duncan snr and David Duncan jnr, discuss the day's work which could be anything from brush heads to barrel bungs for the herring industry or tops and pins for golf clubs.

Slide rules ruled in pre-computer age drawing offices in 1966. Here the staff of George W. Bruce Ltd in Queen's Gardens work on their latest projects which included such prominent buildings as Aberdeen College of Commerce, Elgin Town Hall, Airyhall School and the NORCO building in George Street.

Drama and Tragedy

Top: Photographer John Gallicker's spectacular picture dramatically illustrates the extent of the damage when a southbound goods train was derailed near Stonehaven in January 1966. Following the accident on the Aberdeen-Edinburgh line the fireman prevented a major disaster by dashing along the line to stop another train from ploughing into the wreckage. By laying detonators and waving a red flag, he was able to stop the train with minutes to spare. The derailment, which cut the line with the south, was on a stretch of track which runs through a deep gorge three miles south of Stonehaven. Bottom: Trains start to get through after workmen cleared the line following the crash of the goods train.

A frightened dog negotiates the masses of rubble and splintered wood left behind at Pennan in the aftermath of the great gale of January 1953.

The picturesque hamlet of Crovie, near Banff, suffered major structural damage in the great gale of January 1953.

The appalling damage wreaked on exposed homes on the seafront at Gardenstown, near Macduff, on the night of January 31, 1953 during the worst gale of the century when freak winds up to 108mph battered the area.

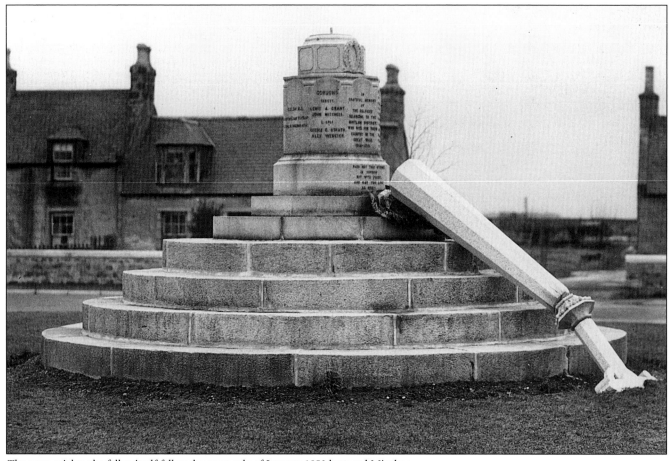

The memorial to the fallen itself fell as the great gale of January 1953 battered Mintlaw.

No. 30,604 206th Year MONDAY FEBRUARY 2 1953 A KEMSLEY NEWSPAPER 2d

THE WEEK-END OF TERROR

The worst gale of the century—a gale that in the North of Scotland started at approximately 5.30 a.m. on Saturday morning — drove a raging tide of terror over the East Coast of England that same Saturday night.

Over 150 people living on the coast between Yorkshire and Kent are known to have been drowned. Over 200 are missing.

People who went to bed shocked by the horror of the loss of the Princess Victoria, with a death roll of 128, woke in the darkness of the night to find flood waters rising rapidly in their homes.

Angry waters raged through peaceful country villages and picturesque seaside towns.

Sea walls were smashed down. Buildings were carried away. Whole communities were cut off. Old and young fled in their night clothes. Those who did not flee in time, or were not able to flee, were drowned.

And all through yesterday emergency services were being mobilised to bring aid to thousands.

In the North of Scotland few living could remember such a gale as blew from 5.30 a.m. to 10.30 p.m. on Saturday— 17 hours with a short lull at 8 p.m.

Several houses on the Banffshire coast were demolished. Great chunks were torn from the roads.

Hundreds of thousands of trees were flattened. Live stock was killed. Telephone, gas and electricity services were disrupted. Road and rail transport was brought to a standstill.

Some fishing boats foundered. Others were torn from their moorings and holed on the rocks.

All day men toiled at the task of restoring electricity supplies, of repairing telephone lines, of clearing trees from roads and railways.

The light loss of life in the North was remarkable. Two Shetland fishermen were drowned. Three men were killed.

Also remarkable was the fact that a stretch of the east side of Britain, from Dundee to Yorkshire, got off comparatively lightly.

In the West the gale that sent the Princess Victoria to her doom left twenty-six drifters smashed on the shore at Ullapool.

In Holland 138 were drowned when the sea broke through dykes on the western seaboard.

It will take months, even years, to redeem the damage wrought by the "hundred Lynmouths" of the week-end.

360 Dead or Missing in Britain's Worst Floods

The worst gale of the century started in the North of Scotland at 5.30pm on Saturday, January 31 and lasted 17 hours. With the wind gusting to 108mph several houses on the Banff coast were demolished and massive chunks torn from the roads. Thousands of trees, including many in Aberdeen parks, were flattened and livestock killed. Telephones, gas and electricity services were disrupted. Road and rail transport were brought to a standstill. Several fishing boats foundered, others were torn from their moorings and holed on the rocks. Twenty-six herring drifters from the North-East were driven ashore at Ullapool. Two Shetland fishermen drowned and three men were killed. All day on Sunday, February 1, workmen toiled to restore electricity supplies, repair telephone lines and clear roads and railways.

One of the lucky ones – an injured workman is carried on a stretcher to a waiting ambulance after being dug out of the wreckage of the Aberdeen University zoology building which collapsed while under construction at the end of October 1966. Five workmen died when the building collapsed in on itself like a pack of cards. Bottom left of the picture is the author and to his right, in the checked hat, is bearded reporter Quentin Clark. They formed part of the team which covered the incident for the *Evening Express* and *The Press and Journal*. Just behind the fireman in the centre of the picture, wearing a light coloured coat, is Dr David Proctor, former head of the Accident and Emergency Department at Woolmanhill, who led the medical team on the scene.

Like a pack of cards the remains of the collapsed Aberdeen University zoology building lie in a pile as firemen and workmen try to reach trapped workmen underneath. The horrific incident was witnessed by two research students, Brian Williamson (22) of Provost Rust Drive and Donald McKerron (23) of Rubislaw Den North, who were in the nearby botany building when the construction collapsed before their eyes.

In September 1968 *Evening Express* photographer John Gallicker took this dramatic shot of a fireman on top of a turntable ladder directing a jet of water on to a spectacular blaze at J. & A. Ogilvie's furniture store in Willowbank Road, Aberdeen. Firemen succeeded in keeping the flames away from the petrol tanks in the Esso filling station next door.

High-perched firemen tackle a spectacular blaze which swept through a paper store in Rose Street, Aberdeen, belonging to Middleton the printers in May 1968. All the company's records dating from 1950 to 1965 were consumed by the flames. The store stood just yards from the site of the firm's former printing works which were destroyed in a £100,000 blaze in 1949.

Firemen carry out mopping up operations after the spectacular blaze which destroyed half the buildings of Aberdeen Combworks in Hutcheon Street in April 1969.

The 1969 fire was the second to hit Aberdeen Combworks in a decade. Here firemen tackle the blaze which badly damaged the works in September 1961.

Flames shoot high into the night sky in May 1963 as historic Seaton House is gutted from end to end. The 17th-century mansion, in the tree-clad polices of Old Seaton, had stood empty since 1956 when Major Hay of Seaton stopped living there, and it became a regular target for vandals.

Seaton House, home to generations of the Hay family until 1956, stands in smoking ruins the morning after a devastating blaze in May 1963, which ended plans to turn the empty mansion into a museum.

Lots of young lads dream of going to sea, but in April 1950 John Guthrie, 13, turned dreams into reality when he sailed off in the Arbroath fishing boat, *Girl Jean*, sparking a major sea and air hunt. The boat is pictured from the air as it makes for Aberdeen, under escort by the Hull trawler, *Reptonian*. Thousands lined the harbour to greet his arrival following his three-day adventure.

The *Blue Crusader*, one of Aberdeen's most advanced trawlers disappeared after sailing from its home port on January 13, 1965 with 13 men on board, under the command of one of the city's most experienced skippers, Fred 'Sunshine' Baker (50). Another vessel, the *Scottish King*, tailed it until evening. Its skipper, Danny McPherson, was the last person to speak to the *Blue Crusader* crew at around 7.30pm on the radio when Skipper Baker said he was heading for the Faroe Islands. A force 10 gale blew up around midnight when Skipper McPherson reckoned the *Crusader* would have been in the teeth of the storm. However, it was not until January 26 that fears arose for the vessel and a full-scale search was mounted. The people of Aberdeen reacted in typical fashion, the Lord Provost's appeal fund-raising more than £25,000 by early February for the families of the crew. There was even a small donation from the inmates of Craiginches Prison. The crew were Colin McKay (15) of Fetterangus who was making his first trip to sea; Hugh McKenzie (49) and John Ronald (40) both fathers of six from Aberdeen; mate Thomas Slater; chief engineer William Anderson (39); second engineer Arthur Duncan (34); Alexander Cruickshank (23); Arthur Forman (43); Alfred Copeland (19), all Aberdeen; David Stanger (19) of Whitecairns; Alex Grubb (23) of Portlethen; and William Reid (37) of Buckie.

The first relic of the *Blue Crusader*, a battered red and blue lifebelt was discovered on the uninhabited Orkney island of Auskerry on February 6, 1965, a week after the alarm was raised for the missing trawler with 13 men on board.

Workmen at Point Law examine a mast, believed to have come from the *Blue Crusader*, picked up a year after the boat, with 13 men on board, disappeared off Orkney in a force 10 gale in January 1965.

In May 1961, the 294-ton trawler, *Red Crusader* left Aberdeen for the fertile fishing grounds around Faroe with a 12-man crew under Skipper Ted Wood whose daredevil exploits earned him the nickname 'Typhoon Ted'. By the first day of June, Ted was more than living up to his reputation when his trawler came under fire from the Danish Navy. At dawn on May 31, a two-man police party boarded the *Red Crusader* from the frigate, *Neils Ebbsen* and ordered him to sail to the Faroese port of Thorshavn to face charges of illegal fishing within the six-mile limit reserved for Faroese boats. Ted told his crew that as his 1958-built vessel could easily outrun the elderly Dane, built in Aberdeen in the 1940s, he was going to make a run for it. When Commodore Eugen Soelling saw the *Crusader* change course he ordered his men to fire a blank shot as a warning. When that failed to impress he opened up with live shells. Bullets and shells hit the bow and radar scanner, but no one on board was injured. Shortly afterwards, the Royal Navy arrived on the scene under orders to escort the *Crusader* to any port she wished. She limped to Aberdeen, where, with the Danish ship anchored six miles offshore, a series of conferences began between officials, lawyers and the crew of the *Crusader*. An independent commission judged that there was no evidence the *Crusader* had fished inside the limit and that Commodore Soelling had exceeded the legitimate use of armed force. The day the findings were published the *Crusader* was back fishing at Faroe, but it was not until January 1963, that it was allowed to land in Faroese ports.

Skipper 'Typhoon' Ted Wood on his return from Faroe after his trawler, *Red Crusader*, was shelled by the Danish Navy for allegedly fishing within Faroese fishing limits in 1961. Ted retired in 1973 and two years later the *Crusader* ran aground in Thurso Bay and was sold for scrap.

Homecomings were never like this – the crew of the *Red Crusader* set off to meet their families from Aberdeen harbour after outrunning the Danish Navy and coming under fire from one of its ships in 1961.

The battered remains of the Longhope Lifeboat berthed at Scrabster Harbour after being towed in by Thurso Lifeboat in March 1969 following the disaster in which seven Orkney crewmen died.

Seven brave Orkney crewmen died when the Longhope Lifeboat from the island of Hoy was overwhelmed by heavy seas while going to the rescue of the Liberian cargo vessel, the *B.B. Irine*, which ran aground on the island of South Ronaldsay on the night of March 17-18 in 1969. Cox Dan Kirkpatrick and his men were laid to rest side by side in South Walls cemetery which overlooks the bleak waters of the Pentland Firth where they perished on their mission of mercy.

Not the best place to land your catch, but that's what the fishermen on board the grounded Aberdeen trawler, *Sturdee*, are doing as it sits high and dry on Aberdeen Beach under the lee of the city's gasworks in October 1955. Eleven fishermen were rescued by Aberdeen Lifeboat when the vessel ran aground on a sandbank in thick fog about 150 yards from the beach. By fine seamanship the lifeboat crew had all the fishermen safely aboard within an hour of the incident. As she manoeuvred alongside they leapt to safety.

November 1952 saw the Aberdeen trawler, *Loch Lomond*, run aground in the Navigation Channel at Aberdeen Harbour. The spectacular sight of the boat being battered against the harbour wall attracted large crowds of onlookers.

The Grimsby trawler, *Lombard*, stuck fast on the sands at the mouth of the Ythan after running aground in February 1957.

The crew of the fishing boat, *Guide Us*, survey the damage after she ran aground on rocks in Greyhope Bay opposite Girdleness Lighthouse at 5am on September 25, 1955.

Photographer Jack Cryle caught the heart-stopping moment when the line parted as the Faroese fishing boat, *Fame*, was being towed into Aberdeen Harbour in January 1959. The trawler's steering had been crippled in huge gales four days earlier and she had been towed 180 miles to Aberdeen through winter gales. As the harbour tug, *Danny*, kept her on a short tow for the entry into port, the swell proved too much for the wire hawser. With the stricken vessel in danger of being smashed against the breakwater, the pilot boat, under the command of George Flett, dashed in to hold her in position until the *Danny* got a new line on board. Jack's memorable picture shows the hawser snaking through the air after it parted with a massive 'crack'.

The Granton trawler, *Contender*, is pictured on the rocks near Cruden Bay after running aground at the mouth of the Ythan in April 1961.

Looking none the worse for their ordeal, the crew of the Aberdeen-built Granton trawler, *Contender*, enjoy a warming cuppa at the Coastguard Station in Cruden Bay after it ran aground at the mouth of the Ythan in April 1961.

The first the crew of the Aberdeen seiner, *Semnos II*, knew they had run aground at Forvie Sands at the mouth of the Ythan in December 1966, was when they heard a grinding sound. Skipper Jack Smith ordered the setting off of distress flares and called Stonehaven Radio. The water was too shallow for the Aberdeen Lifeboat, *Ramsay Dyce*, to go to her assistance and the crew had to be rescued by breeches buoy through broken surf. She was refloated after a fortnight.

Members of the crew of the fishing boat, *Semnos II*, relax in the Royal Mission for Deep Sea Fishermen in Aberdeen after their ordeal. They are, left to right, Francis Slater, William Smith, Russell Falconer, James Findlay, Skipper Jack Smith, and James Mair. On the left is Superintendent Jack Moore of the Mission.

Rescue heroes are honoured for their brilliant lifesaving feat. Albert Hendry (left), No 1 of the Collieston Coastguard Rescue Company and John Troup (second left), No 1 of the Belhelvie Company, received the Board of Trade Shield for the best wreck service of the year on behalf of their Coastguard Rescue Companies from Chief Inspector of Coastguards, Commander P. Bartlett (centre) at a dinner in the New Inn Hotel at Ellon. The companies gained the award for their rescue of six men by breeches buoy from the stranded fishing boat, *Semnos II*, near the mouth of the Ythan in December 1966.

Another victim of the Forvie Sands near Newburgh, the Fraserburgh fishing boat, *Stephens*, lies badly holed after running aground in November 1956. The boat was returning from the East Anglian fishing grounds where she had established herself as joint leader in the Prunier Trophy competition when she ran aground. The crew was rescued by the Collieston and Belhelvie lifesaving teams using a breeches buoy. At the subsequent Ministry of Transport enquiry, Sheriff Hamilton and three assessors found the stranding was the fault of skipper Fred Stephen and ordered his certificate to be suspended for six months. The court also found the mate, Joseph Fraser of Fraserburgh was also at fault and recommended his certificate should be suspended for the same period.

A dinghy from the Russian cargo vessel, *Krymov*, which ran aground in a storm on Murcar Sands just north of Aberdeen in March 1956, tries to reach shore but is nearly overturned by the violent seas. The three men on board were forced to return to the ship.

Stepping off the dinghy which ferried them to shore, members of the crew of the Russian steamer, *Krymov*, pick their way across stepping stones to the beach at Murcar in March 1956. The remainder of the crew wait their turn by the rope ladder down the side of the ship.

As the storm lashes the Russian cargo ship, *Krymov*, stuck fast on Murcar Sands in March 1956, coastguards fire a lifeline and the crew make it fast.

Six of the seven-man crew of the Fraserburgh lifeboat perished when it capsized at the entrance to Fraserburgh Harbour on February 9, 1953. Watched by hundreds of people, the lifeboat, the *John and Charles Kennedy*, was assisting fishing boats entering the port through heavy seas when tragedy struck. She had just escorted the yawl, *Good Way*, into harbour and went out again to meet the *Harvest Reaper*. But the skipper of the fishing boat decided to head for Macduff. The lifeboat was returning to harbour when a massive, unbroken wave caught her at the harbour mouth, capsizing her. Little could be done to help the crew, some of whom were seen swimming for the shore. Coxwain Andrew Ritchie was 20 yards from shore when he was struck on the head by a piece of wood and his strength gave out. Crowds gather in silent tribute.

Photographer Jim Love and *Evening Express* fishing correspondent Arthur Middleton were on the spot when a Royal Navy bomb disposal team dealt with a live World War Two German mine brought up in the fishing nets of the Aberdeen trawler, *Donside*, in August 1962. Also on board were the trawler's skipper, James Baxter and crew members, George Murray, mate, and chief engineer William Mitchell. The most dangerous moment came when the navymen had to lift the mine from the deck and sling it over the side with a bed of nets between it and the side of the boat. Before it was lowered 100ft to the sea bed two miles from shore, the mine, capable of flattening an entire street, was given a 'necklace' of explosives. When the mine was exploded using a long fuse, the tremor was so great it was felt by people walking on the promenade three miles away.

Devotion to duty earned *Evening Express* photographer, David Sutherland, a top award for this dramatic picture of the Lossiemouth seine netter, *Devotion*, aground on rocks at Pennan in August 1960. His picture won a place in the British Press Pictures of the Year – the Blue Riband in press photography – organised by *Encyclopaedia Britannica*. Four of the crew lost their lives in the incident. David recalls setting off from Pennan in the editorial car with driver Willie McDonald. No one in the village knew exactly where the wreck was and it was suggested he go by boat. With no craft available for an hour and his deadline looming, he set off by road, down a rough track through fields so rough that a large rock damaged the car's sump. The journey was completed on foot and David got his picture by lying flat over a cliff, with Willie hanging on to his ankles.

Evening Express and *Press and Journal* photographer David Sutherland who risked life and limb to get his memorable, award-winning picture of the stricken fishing boat, *Devotion*, by hanging over a cliff with driver Willie McDonald hanging on to his ankles.

'Willie Mac', one of the great characters of Aberdeen Journals in the Fifties and Sixties. Willie McDonald was 37 years with the company and was a familiar face on the newspaper delivery routes to Deeside and Inverness before becoming editorial driver, taking reporters to assignments all over the city and North-East, sometimes in atrocious weather conditions. The fact that he was one of the North-East's first advanced drivers was greatly appreciated as he negotiated snow drifts and blizzards to help reporters get their stories and photographers get their pictures.

In Sickness and in Health

The Queen chats with Miss Violet Maltman, matron at the City Hospital during the grim weeks of the typhoid epidemic of May and June 1964. Also in the picture are Dr James Brodie, the hospital's laboratory director, and Lord Provost Norman Hogg. In 1983 Miss Maltman died after being knocked down by a car near her home in Clifton Road.

Lord Provost Norman Hogg says a big thank you to Andy Stewart and the rest of his show's cast, for cheering up the citizens of Aberdeen in August 1964 after the typhoid epidemic. Pictured left to right are Max Kay, the Lady Provost, Diane Taylor, Andy, Sally Logan, the Lord Provost and Ian Powrie.

The city says thank you to its health workers. More than 1,000 doctors, nurses, health workers, clerks and others who helped fight the typhoid epidemic were guests at a civic reception in the Beach Ballroom.

Even the *Evening Express*'s Wee Alickie was recruited to help drive home the message of personal hygiene during the typhoid epidemic.

Disinfectant and personal hygiene were of paramount importance when handling foodstuffs during the typhoid epidemic.

Hello Grandma. A young victim of the typhoid epidemic has to chat to his granny through the window of the City Hospital.

The Queen meets Nurse Margaret Pauline during her visit to Aberdeen to sound the 'all clear' in the typhoid epidemic.

Evening Express

No. 26,878 (EST 1879) SATURDAY MAY 30 1964 4d

LATE EXTRA

SHINNIE for SELF-DRIVE CARS

What YOU can do

- Wash your hands carefully after using the toilet and before handling food.
- Use individual towels or paper towels.
- In food shops, etc., insist on scrupulous food hygiene.
- Take a few tissues with you if you go to eat in a restaurant to dry your hands after washing and immediately before food.
- Use foods deemed safe and avoid potentially dangerous foods.
- DON'T eat pre-cooked cold meat, cream cakes and salads.
- REMEMBER: Soap and nailbrush are the best weapons against typhoid.

TODAY'S TOTAL

141 CONFIRMED **42** SUSPECT

How the germ spreads

- Symptoms appear after 10-15 days' incubation and include persistent and severe headache, weakness and languor, abdominal pain and intestinal upset, temperature rises bit by bit and face becomes flushed and stomach enlarges.
- The germ comes from (a) the patient, (b) a recovered patient or (c) a healthy carrier (some people become carriers without obvious illness).
- The germ reaches the next person by passing from the discharges of a case or carrier, for example excreta, urine, blood or sweat, to the mouth of the next victim.

NOW A BELEAGUERED CITY

A fleet of ambulances outside Tor-na-Dee Hospital this morning. Patients were being moved from the hospital to make room for typhoid cases.

Bully: MPs table host of queries

As Aberdeen steeled itself to the mounting total of typhoid cases, MPs today gave notice of questions suggesting a flare-up in the Commons over the release of years-old bully beef by the Ministry of Food.

Mr Kenneth Robinson, 'shadow' Minister of Health, is to question the Minister of Health when Parliament assembles on Tuesday, about allegations that the Government were still releasing contaminated corned beef.

City social life takes knock as events called off

SOCIAL life in Aberdeen has been given a big knock with news of further events postponed or cancelled because of the typhoid outbreak.

Quarter million people at risk

ABERDEEN is now a beleaguered city. That was the description of it given today by Dr Ian A. G. MacQueen, city medical officer of health, as he made a dramatic appeal for action to stem the second major wave of typhoid. His advice was:

- DON'T leave the city if you are an Aberdonian.
- DON'T come to Aberdeen unless it is absolutely necessary.

Where the suspect tin came from

ON the source of the present outbreak, Dr MacQueen said:

'Stay away decision will kill trade'

SHOPKEEPERS in Aberdeen were stunned by the news that summer visitors had been told to cancel their holidays in Aberdeen.

Ballroom closed

Brisk

Ghost town

Second major wave

How the numbers have risen

HOW the numbers of CONFIRMED cases have risen since the outbreak started:—

Thursday night	11
Friday night	17
Saturday night	21
Sunday night	48
Monday night	74
Tuesday night	89
Wednesday night	97
Thursday night	112
Last night	136

Broch water —visit ban

ALL access to Fraserburgh's main water supply was forbidden today after two car loads of Aberdeen people were seen fishing in the dam.

WILL open

SPECIFY PERIOD, HE SAYS

University will remain open

Volunteer typists

Disappointment . . . a little girl reads the notice on the door of the Civic Arts Centre.

RACING RESULTS

How the *Evening Express* told the people of Aberdeen that they were now officially a beleaguered city. Medical officer of health Dr Ian MacQueen warned Aberdonians not to leave the city and appealed to outsiders to stay away unless their visit was absolutely necessary.

Aberdeen turns out to greet the Queen and say a heartfelt thank you for her decision to visit Aberdeen after the typhoid epidemic in 1964 and let the world know the city was safe to visit. Following the announcement that the outbreak was over, the Queen's private secretary contacted Lord Provost Norman Hogg and told him she would like to visit the city the next evening. A 24-hour action plan, which included the *Evening Express* and *The Press and Journal* letting the people know she was coming, was launched with the result that more than 40,000 people turned out to welcome her. As she prepared to leave Joint Station at the end of her visit she told Lord Provost Hogg, 'Now I know what's it's like to be The Beatles'. For five long weeks the city had been in the grip of the epidemic with more than 400 people quarantined in hospital wards. The outbreak was met with worldwide hysteria. Boarding houses, hotels and holiday camps were out of bounds to any visitors from Aberdeen. And despite the long, hot summer, no one came on holiday. Aberdeen was effectively a ghost town, struck by what appeared to the outside world to be a medieval plague. The epidemic peaked in late May and early June, but of the hundreds admitted to hospital only one elderly woman died. On June 18, Aberdeen got the all clear but the stigma remained until the Queen's visit relieved the city a week later.

This says it all about Aberdeen's first Bon Accord Festival Parade in 1964. Having got the all clear from the typhoid epidemic the city staged a fortnight of celebrations with the parade as the highlight. This fun entry from the City Hospital, where typhoid patients were isolated, could hardly have failed to pick up a prize.

Much-loved medical practitioner Dr Mary Esslemont had surgeries in the west end and Torry. A gynaecologist at the free dispensary in the Guestrow, she became the first woman president of the Medico-Chirurgical Society in 1957. She was the first woman chairman of the British Medical Association, later becoming a life president, having been elected a fellow in 1959. She became a fellow of the Royal College of General Practitioners in 1969 and received a CBE in 1955. A JP she served on the University Court throughout the Fifties and Sixties, until 1974 and was awarded the freedom of the city in 1981. Here she is pictured with leading Indian medical authority Dr B. Mukerji at a reception in the Town House in August 1963.

Professor Sir Dugald Baird and his wife, Lady May, made history in 1966 when they became the first husband and wife to be made Freemen of Aberdeen. An internationally-renowned obstetrician, his revolutionary approach to medical research and practice placed him and Aberdeen on the medical map. Regius Professor of Obstetrics and Gynaecology from 1937 until 1965, he championed what he called the Fifth Freedom – a woman's right to be free from the tyranny of excessive fertility. As well as supporting the contraceptive pill, it was his policy from the late Thirties to grant abortion on social grounds. He also pioneered the screening of North-East women for cervical cancer. By 1966 almost every married woman under 70 in Aberdeen had had at least one smear test in the past 10 years. His work at the Foresterhill Research Centre on a study of children from pregnancy through infancy to adolescence was the only one of its kind with continuous records. Lady May was chairwoman of the North-East Regional Hospital Board for nearly 20 years, a town councillor and a Governor of the BBC in Scotland. Sir Dugald died in 1989 three years after his wife. Sir Dugald and Lady Baird on the right of the picture wave to the crowds after the Freedom ceremony. Also in the picture are Lord Strathclyde, who was also made a Freeman, and Lord Provost Norman Hogg, left.

Blue Skies and Grey Days

They certainly knew how to build snowmen in 1963. Resplendent in woolly hat and scarf this magnificent snowman, complete with snowboots, towered over Westholme Avenue in Aberdeen's West End after heavy snowfalls in January.

These two youngsters take advantage of heavy snowfalls in Aberdeen in 1968 to hit the slopes on their home-made sledge.

Skating on a frozen Duthie Park pond in 1969.

No need for anti-freeze to get the milk delivered in the winter of 1965. Here driver Alex Will 'reins supreme' on Aberdeen's Great Northern Road at the end of his morning delivery of doorstep pintas.

Winter takes a grip on North-East roads in February 1963, but the blizzards are no match for the crew of this snow plough which spews tons of snow on to the roadside.

Brrr! It was one of the whitest Januaries Aberdeen had seen for years in 1958. But the city was coping better than ever with the worst winter could throw at it with the introduction of a new snow plough. Here it is working in conjunction with a council lorry to clear the snow in Union Street at the junction with Market Street.

A farmer does it the hard way, clearing a path through the snow for his tractor at Banks Farm, Fyvie, during the heavy blizzards of February 1963.

The light catches the delicate tracery of snow on the buildings around Union Terrace Gardens in January 1963. The fairy-tale scene was captured by photographer Gordon Bissett, whose caption suggested that in future years the council might consider creating an ice skating rink in the gardens during winter. Gordon had to wait until the late Nineties to see his dream come true.

Buses find difficulty negotiating the Mid-Stocket Road hill near Mile-End School after heavy snowfalls in February 1965.

Phew, what a scorcher! Some seek the shade of trees while others soak up the lunchtime sun in Union Terrace Gardens as Aberdeen basked in the warmest day of the year on August 2, 1964. Thousands flocked to the beaches and parks all over the North-East.

Anderson Drive in all its glory in the summer of 1968 with the thousands of roses which helped make Aberdeen one of the finest floral cities in Britain.

Young Robert Leiper's mum would have had plenty to say about his soaked shirt and pants when he and June Homer decided to cool off in the fountain at the Victoria Park on a sweltering July day in 1955.

The deck chairs are out and Aberdonians relax in the sun at Hazlehead Park in 1961. Families enjoy a cup of tea and a snack under the sunshades at the restaurant while a queue waits patiently for ice cream.

Temperatures rocketed in Aberdeen in the summer of 1967. Here youngsters cool off by paddling in the burn in a game of follow my leader at the Westburn Park in early July.

Glorious sunshine marks the end of another successful harvest at Dalmaik Farm at Drumoak, near Aberdeen in 1965.

Out came the sun and out came the crowds at Aberdeen Beach in 1966. By then the former Beach Pavilion had become The Gaiety and boy met girl in the popular Holiday Inn where the juke box was never silent between opening and closing time. Mum, Dad and the kids enjoyed an ice cream or a cuppa at the Inversnecky Café, the Pavilion Café or The Washington, while families on the lower prom and sands sought refreshment at the two handy kiosks. On the right is one of several bright red weighing machines whose giant needles pointed painfully to those extra pounds that had been piled on over the summer.

A sight never to be seen again. A heatwave brings out the crowds in their thousands to Aberdeen Beach in July 1966. A few dozen brave the icy waters of the North Sea, but most prefer to relax in deck chairs or on their towels on the sands. On the right of the picture are the two rows of chalets rented out by the town council during the summer. Families would spend long summer days there cooking on a primus stove and relaxing in their own fenced off stretch of beach.

A heat haze hangs over Aberdeen Beach on a Sunday afternoon in 1966. Cars line the prom nose to tail while sunbathers enjoy a picnic on the grass just to the north of the Beach Ballroom.

A couple enjoy the sun under the twin spires of St Machar's Cathedral at Seaton Park in August 1969.

Women and children first – rescuers wade through the flood waters at Maryculter after the Dee burst its banks during the flash floods of November 6, 1951.

Boating down Anderson Drive, Aberdeen after the flash floods of November 1951. November 6 was the day it was easier to take a boat down Anderson Drive in Aberdeen than a car. After 24 hours of solid rain the Walker Dam, near Hazlehead, burst its banks and, despite the efforts of firemen to pump it away at 1,000 gallons a minute, the drains could not cope. Four feet of water flooded surrounding houses. At Maryculter, the River Dee burst its banks forcing caravan owners and those living nearby to abandon their homes, wading through fields up to their waists in water. The surf lifeboat was called out but gave up when fences and other debris fouled its propellers. A shallow salmon cobble continued the rescue operation. More than 600 workers at Mugiemoss Mill got a half-day off when the Don overflowed and flooded the turbines. Work also was curtailed at Stoneywood Mill.

Happy Days

Go-Go Girls come to Aberdeen in 1966 with the opening of the controversial new disco, The Place, in Rose Street by brothers Brian and Paul Waldman. The former Melville Church at the corner of Skene Street opened with a claimed 3,250 members to a storm of criticism from councillors, in particular Mrs Ellen Williamson, who warned it could lead to the circulation of pep pills. The club closed after less than a year.

Some boys never grow up. These old boys' model yachts present a magnificent sight – one that Aberdonians near tire of seeing. Generations of enthusiasts have been sailing their yachts at the Duthie Park pond just as these weekend sailors did in 1969.

The crowds turn out for the switch-on of the Christmas lights in Aberdeen in 1965 and Rudolph the Red Nosed Reindeer adds a festive touch to the parade down Union Street which marked the colourful occasion.

The man who brought the joy of learning to fly Aberdeen, Peter Forbes, pictured after setting up Pegasus Flying Club in December 1969 alighting from one of the club's two aircraft. The former Perth dry cleaner gave up the family business to start the enterprise with his second-hand Cessna 150 trainer and an old caravan on the west side of the airport. Rejected by the RAF as unsuitable to fly, the wartime paratrooper charged clients £8 an hour – and such was the interest he had a queue of 14 would-be pilots on his opening day. His first clients included a clerk, a baker, lorry driver, company directors a nurse and a racehorse owner.

Northfield's Beehive Club even had its own pop group, The Squeeze, made up entirely of members. Here its vocalist James Peacock gives it his all in November 1966.

The Jack Sinclair Band and the Queen's Cross Dancers create a real Scottish sensation in the glorious setting of Union Terrace Gardens at the start of the Festival of Bon Accord in August 1967.

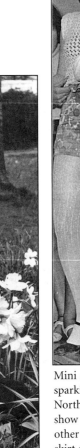

These leggy lovelies took the judges' eye at a mini-skirt competition held by Fettercairn Entertainments Committee at a dance in the village hall in January 1967. Winner was Gail Milne (centre) of the Central Hotel, Edzell. Second place went to Glenda Mitchell (left) of High Street, Laurencekirk, and third place was won by Alice Pirie, of Durie Place, Edzell.

It was a fair double for 20-year-old hairdresser Doreen Malcolm of Balgownie Crescent, Aberdeen, in 1969 when she became Miss Evening Express and Aberdeen's Festival Queen.

Mini skirts were all the rage in 1966 sparking competitions all over the North-East. Here two of the best show a clean pair of heels to the other girls at Rothienorman's mini-skirt competition in December 1966. Wilma Lyttel, a waitress at the Huntly Hotel took the title of best looking girl in a mini-skirt. On her left is Sheila Taylor of Wartle, who was the girl with the shortest mini-skirt.

Bon Accord Festival Queen Kathleen Spence and Councillor Alex Collie break up with laughter at his unsuccessful attempts to find a resting place for her crown on her high hairdo during the crowning ceremony at Aberdeen Beach Ballroom in July 1965.

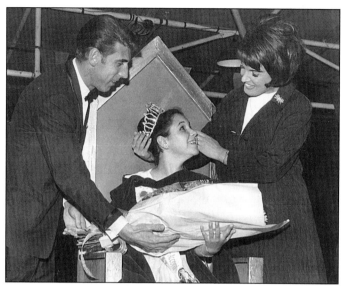

Eighteen-year-old Judith Crighton of Countesswells Crescent, Aberdeen, was the judges' choice for Aberdeen's Festival of Bon Accord Queen in 1967. Judith entered for a dare and was chosen from a total of 12 finalists. She is pictured here being crowned by singer Moira Anderson while comedian Rikki Fulton hands over a bouquet.

Lovely Sylvia Lamont, of Glenbervie Road, Aberdeen, is crowned Aberdeen's Floral Queen in February 1966 by the outgoing queen, Mrs J. Winning, at the St Valentine's Mod Ball in the Beach Ballroom. A pupil of Aberdeen High School for Girls, Sylvia was chosen from a short-list of six girls.

Head of the School of Architecture Stanley Wilkinson is given the enviable task of crowning the 1966 Spirit of the Arts, Jean Whyte, 20 a third year student of physiotherapy, at the Beach Ballroom.

Gladys Wilson smiles for the *Evening Express* after being voted Spirit of the Arts in 1961.

Grampian Television personality Douglas Kynoch congratulates Johanna Allan, Mill of Nethermill, Pennan, after he had chosen her as Miss Fortnightly 1965 at a dance at Fortnightly Hall, Nairn.

Grampian TV Personality of 1966, Jimmy Spankie, is congratulated after receiving his trophy by clerkesses Elizabeth Raitt, left, and Maureen Stephen, at the Queen's Cross Studios. The 30-year-old host of programmes such as *Sportscope* and *Cairngorm Ski*, who topped the viewers' popularity poll to win the award, began his career with Grampian in 1961.

Helping decorate the Beach Ballroom for the Arts Ball in 1969 are, left to right, Mhairi Taylor, Helen Macrae, Spirit of the Arts Carole Moulsdale and Mary MacLeod.

Two well-known personalities formed a lasting partnership in December 1964. Grampian Television presenter June Imray, better known to Aberdonians as the Torry Quine, married Gerry Davis, whose nostalgia programme, *The Way We Were*, proved extremely popular with North-East viewers over the years.

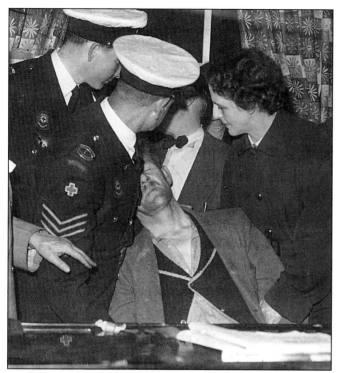

On the ball at the snooker table in Hayton Community Centre in February 1968. Aiming to pot a red is John Matthew. Cueing to take their turn are left to right Alex Rae, Norman Cruickshank, Billy Rae and Andrew Henderson.

End of the line for Syncopating Sandy as he slumps into the arms of first-aid men at the end of his world record beating 157-hour piano playing marathon at the Music Hall. The Bolton engineer managed to tinkle out the National Anthem before exhaustion took over. The 1,000-strong crowd who witnessed the finale, burst into *For He's a Jolly Good Fellow* as he was helped form the Round Room. More than 36,000 people paid to see Sandy during his marathon.

After money was stolen from the 62 Club in 1964, members rallied round to raise more cash. And one way of doing it was with a successful folk song session for guests.

Members of the 62 Club hold an all-night Christmas Vigil outside the West Church of St Andrew to raise funds for the Phoenix Club for the Disabled in December 1964.

Star performers at Aberdeen Zoo were these mountain lion cubs which proved a major draw after the re-opening of the zoo following its temporary closure during the height of the 1967 foot and mouth epidemic.

Back in captivity at Aberdeen Zoo in March 1967 after going walkabout for three months is Syrup the porcupine. Welcoming her back is zoo manager George Leslie a few hours after a 3am phone call from the police telling him she had been discovered at the back of the Den Wood beside Countesswells Road. Though it never quite achieved the worldwide fame of Goldie, the flyaway London golden eagle, the saga of Syrup created quite a stir in Aberdeen.

When is a badger more of a Beatle – when it's called Ringo. And that's just what happened to this new addition to Aberdeen Zoo in 1964. The rare West African honey badger was presented to the North-East of Scotland Zoological Society for the new zoo. The badger was taken in as a pup by a Scottish family in Gambia after its mother had been shot. Raised like a dog, it was christened Ringo by the couple's daughter before they discovered it was really a female. Ringo is pictured with Dr Lil de Kok who looked after it until it was ready to move into the zoo.

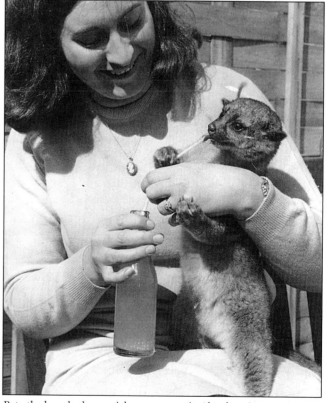

Beta the bear had a special engagement in Aberdeen in August 1966. The South American bundle of fun travelled 7,000 miles to Aberdeen to undertake a special mission. Beta was a highly unusual engagement present to 19-year-old student Anne Morgan from her fiancé, Barry Erskine, a second officer in the Merchant Navy. For a while Beta romped around the family home in King Street, climbing and clambering everywhere. But the pint-sized Peruvian could not be house trained, so became a welcome arrival at the Hazlehead Zoo.

Who's getting the next round, then? These two lads can scarcely believe the monkey business that's going on in the Tivoli Bar. The thirsty chimp in the straw hat was enjoying a quick pint during the interval of the Christmas show at the city's best-loved music hall in 1952.

Movie buff Humphrey the chimp gate-crashed the Odeon Cinema Children's Club in April 1969 to try on the Easter bonnets created by the kids in a Saturday morning competition.

This handsome bird became quite a personality in Aberdeen in 1950. Walking along Aberdeen Beach one blustery March day Mr Edward Mitchell of Powis Place thought he saw a penguin walking out of the sea towards him. As it got closer Mr Mitchell recognised it as a guillemot, which started following him like a little dog. Mr Mitchell picked up the incredibly tame bird and took it home, but later released it for fear it would pine, and because of the vast quantities of salt and fish it needed in its daily diet.

Chubby Checker is king – and these fans say 'Let's Twist Again' at the Beach Ballroom during a twist contest in 1962.

Enjoying their break, this happy group of workmates pose for the photographer on the roof of Farquhar and Gill's paint factory in St Paul's Street, Aberdeen, in the Fifties. The girls, who worked on the production line, got together 40 years later for an emotional reunion.

Over she goes. These youngsters are having a high old time at a rock 'n' roll competition at the Music Hall in 1956.

Something to blaw about – prize winners display their trophies at the City of Aberdeen Ladies Pipe Band dinner and presentation of prizes in the Palace Restaurant in June 1967. Highlight of the night was when band secretary William Munro presented the band with the Miller Trophy won at Forfar earlier in the year, the first time the trophy had been won by a band outside the Forfar area.

Aberdeen Ladies Pipe Band, resplendent in their magnificent uniforms, with their prizes in 1968.

Only three young lads had the nerve to join the girls on the boards at Aberdeen Beach for a rock'n' roll competition on a hot July day in 1960. The girl dancing in the centre of the picture is wearing the full petticoats under her skirt which every girl who loved to jive at the Beach Ballroom seemed to wear in those days. Buses line the prom to take the sunseekers back to the town centre.

It's the Beatles era and everyone reckons they can be the next George, John, Ringo or Paul. Budding new Beatles battle it out at Aberdeen Beach in 1965 in a pop competition. The winners, pictured here, are an Aberdeen University pop group, The Patter Merchants. Runners up were The Delinquents.

Not the warmest of summer days but that didn't deter families in 1964 from heading for Aberdeen Beach for a fun day out. Wrapped up warm in hats and blue trench coats these smiling kids are having the time of their lives on the rides at the Carnival while mums and dads look on.

Anyone for tennis. The racquet is as big as wee Gillian Fordyce. But she can't wait to show her mum that she's a future Wimbledon prospect during a sweltering hot day at Aberdeen beach in June 1958.

In 1965 there was an impression that the appeal of the Timmer Market was beginning to wane, but you wouldn't have noticed it from this turn-out, though sparkling sunshine probably helped boost the crowds.

The Scourge of the Timmer Market in the Fifties and Sixties. The dreaded pea shooter sold like hot cakes, but while stallholders were happy with the profits, shoppers who felt the sting of dry barley on the back of their necks, were less than impressed. Here a couple of youngsters get in some target practice around the stalls in 1962.

Not even a pair of tooteroos can rouse two-year-old Gordon Slessor of Castle Street, from his slumber at the Timmer Market in 1967. But Kenneth, 4, and Michele Smith, 2, of Arnage Gardens, clearly think the market is a blast.

Stall holder Stuart Kidd has these two youngsters mystified with his dancing dolls at the Timmer Market in 1969. Dawn (3) and David (4) Barclay of Kincorth Crescent are clearly impressed.

Two-year-old John Gordon takes a keen interest in the handmade wooden lorry at the opening of the Timmer Market in August 1956. With him is his mum Mrs J. Gordon and Mrs J. Haugh, both of Willowbank Road.

Open air draughts and Aberdeen's Union Terrace Gardens went together like coffee and cream in the Fifties and Sixties. Here John Pirie (right), Aberdeen draughts champion, takes on all comers in August 1961.

Who could forget the smiling face of the North-East's couthiest broadcaster, John Mearns. The star of Grampian Television's *Ingle Neuk* was equally well-known as the star of another series – Aberdeen's annual festival celebrations – for several years. Here John is having a go with the kids at the donkey derby at the Queen's Links on a sunny June day in 1968.

It looks like the entire city has turned out to cheer the floats in the Aberdeen Festival Parade as it makes its way down Union Street from its start point in Carden Place to the Beach Boulevard in June 1968.

Aberdeen Sea Cadets lead the way as Aberdonians and holidaymakers turned out in force to watch the Festival of Bon Accord parade down Union Street in July 1964.

No bones about it. These revellers are having a great time at the kipper barbecue at Aberdeen Fish Market during the finale of the 1967 Festival of Bon Accord.

Youngsters enjoy a rock session at Aberdeen Beach during the 1968 Aberdeen Festival celebrations.

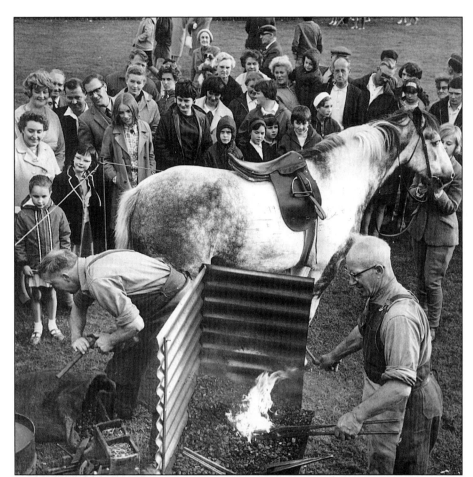

A big draw at the 1968 Aberdeen festival celebrations at Hazlehead was this demonstration of horse shoeing by Mr Fred Innes, left and Mr A. Melvin. Paying 'neigh' attention to what's going on is Shannon from Nigg.

Getting in the festive spirit, James Sim of South Constitution Street joins bemused youngsters for a beat session during the finale of the Festival of Bon Accord in Aberdeen in August 1967.

Fascinated spectators look on as Bill Forbes fillets freshly landed fish at the kipper barbecue and scampi fish fry, which formed the finale of the Festival of Bon Accord at Aberdeen Fish Market in August 1966.

Keen dressmakers at Hayton Community Centre in 1968. On the left of our picture keeping the knitting needles going while they learn, are Mary McIntosh and Mary Downie. Their fellow seamstresses are Helen Smith, Mary Lobban, Helen Henderson, Margaret Pettifer, Hilda Graham and Lilly Miazek.

The lights are low but hopes are high as late night gamblers make their bets at the roulette wheel in the Blue Chip Casino in the Hardgate in May 1964.

Councillor Tom Scott Sutherland, chairman of the city's first bowling alley, Granite Bowl in Loch Street, collects his shilling bet from former Scottish football referee Peter Craigmyle after he threw the first bowl to celebrate the opening in 1962. Tom had bet Peter £5 to a shilling that he would not get a strike in the first three bowls.

Ten-pin bowling came to Aberdeen in December 1962 with the opening of the city's first bowling alley, the Granite Bowl in George Street. The first teams to take to the 16 lanes were given special coaching organised by the *Evening Express*. The night produced the city's first champion, bus conductor Bob Stuart of Deevale Gardens, who scored 115 points.

The sun comes out for Keith Show in August 1969, and this young competitor steals a march on his fellow racers at the start of the sulky donkey race.

Rounding the bend at breakneck speed in the handicap trot, these riders thrill the crowds watching the afternoon's sport programme at Seafield Park during the 1966 Keith Show.

Mums and dads of boys from the 67th Boys Brigade Company having fun at their Burns Supper in the Embassy Rooms, Woodside in 1969.

My wife, Una Chalmers, at three years of age looking less than confident as she makes friends with Muffin the Mule in coronation year 1953 at the beach carnival.

Enjoying a day out to Hazlehead in 1958 included getting your picture taken with the stuffed bear at the park entrance. Here mother and daughter Beatrice and Kathleen Allan pose for the photographer like hundreds of others did before and after them.

Staff and guests of Aberdeen Journals Ltd enjoying a great night out at their annual dinner dance in 1961.

Tradition and Ceremony

The beautiful three-masted schooner, *Prince Louis*, training ship of the Outward Bound Moray Sea School, proved a big attraction when she berthed at Aberdeen Harbour in October 1956. The schooner was on a five-day visit to show the people in the North-East the work of the school. The vessel had a crew of 30 including 24 boys.

What a magnificent sight – the Sail Training Association schooner, *Malcolm Miller*, spreads canvass as she cruises off Aberdeen on her sailing trials in February 1968. Photographer Mike Stephen's memorable picture was taken from the deck of the Fraserburgh-registered seine netter, *Ocean Searcher*.

Thirteen-year-old Carol Sim faces the piping judges for the first time in the juvenile piping competition at Aberdeen Highland Games in September 1965.

Lady Miller smashes the traditional bottle of champagne on the bows of the Sail Training Association schooner, *Malcolm Miller*, sending her on her way to an illustrious career in 1966 that was to last until almost the end of the century. The £175,000 ship was built at the Torry shipyard of John Lewis and Sons Ltd. Her scratch crew included sea cadets, sea scouts and yachting enthusiasts. In command was Captain Glyn Griffiths, an experienced ocean going yachtsman, who formerly served on the Association's *Sir Winston Churchill*.

These youngsters show how the Highland Fling should be danced in the 8-11 class at Aberdeen Highland Games at Hazlehead in September 1964.

Dancing the Sean Truibhs at Aberdeen's first Highland Games at Hazlehead in September 1960 are Douglas Duncan, Moira Graham and Eileen Cheyne.

Piper Nessie Lindsay strikes a blow for the ladies at Aberdeen's first Highland Games at Hazlehead in 1960. Nessie is pictured here with the other competitors and judges in the Pibroch competition.

American Big Bill Bangert, Mayor of Champ, Missouri, was a favourite of the crowds on the Highland Games circuit in the Sixties. Here he dashes to a waiting car on the last lap of his transatlantic journey to take part in the Aboyne Games in September 1969. Seeing him off is John Swanson, pilot of the Auster light aircraft which flew him from Prestwick to Dinnet airfield.

Darn it! Once again Big Bill Bangert finds the caber a handful, failing to make the toss on yet another visit to Deeside. The Duke of Edinburgh took delight in offering Bill a few tips on technique at Braemar.

Kilt flying, English athlete Arthur Rowe tosses the caber to win the world championship at Aberdeen Highland Games in June 1968.

A mighty Yank – but not good enough. The Revd Arnold Pope from America shows great technique but not enough muscle to flip the caber over during the world championships at Aberdeen Highland Games in June 1969.

Former Partick Thistle goalie John Feebairn putts the heavy shot at Aberdeen Highland Games in 1963. Waiting their turn are fellow heavies, left to right, Henry Gray, George Charles and Bill Anderson.

Heave! And Strathdeveron tug o' war team rise to the occasion at Aberdeen Highland Games at Hazlehead in September 1962.

They're off! Runners make a flying start in the 100 yards event at Aberdeen Highland Games in August 1963.

Eyes right as the bands take part in the traditional March Past during Aberdeen Highland Games at Hazlehead in June 1967. Taking the salute is Major David Gordon.

Overshadowed by the great Deeside spectacle, the Braemar Gathering, Donside's smaller Lonach Games is nevertheless an equally colourful and popular annual event. Here the Lonach Highlanders march round the games field at Bellabeg, Strathdon in August 1954. Leading the march is Col. Sir John Forbes, sixth baronet of Newe, patron of the Lonach Highland and Friendly Society, founded in 1823 on the creation of Sir Charles Forbes as first baronet.

The young Prince Charles shares a joke with his grandmother, the Queen Mother, as Princess Anne concentrates on the sports at the Braemar Gathering in 1957.

The Prince of Wales gets in step with President Eisenhower during an after-breakfast stroll on the lawn at Balmoral Castle in August 1959. The American president was saying goodbye to the royal family after a week-end stay. Ever the perfect hostess, the Queen stood at the gates of the castle to wave him goodbye as he drove to Aberdeen Airport with the Duke of Edinburgh. At the Pass of Ballater he was greeted by children with a huge banner proclaiming 'We Like Ike'.

Provost J.P. Craig sees Prince Charles and Princess Anne off from Ballater Station in May 1955 on their way with one of the royal corgis to Balmoral.

The Lord Lieutenant of Aberdeenshire, the 2nd Marquess of Aberdeen, greets the Queen as she arrives with a dashing Duke of Edinburgh at the Braemar Games in September 1954, the year after her coronation.

No fewer than 10 pipe bands combined to create this stirring sight and sound at the Queen's Links during the Festival of Bon Accord in August 1966.

Pipers and drummers take a breather during the parade of the animals at Turriff Show in 1969. Most of Scotland's agricultural shows were blessed with good weather that sunny year and at Turriff it was a scorcher!

Country comes to town in February 1962, for the Aberdeen Spring Show at the Kittybrewster Mart. These farmers are looking at the latest hi-tech equipment in the implements and machinery section.

Knowing eyes pick out the best at Kittybrewster Mart. Aberdeen Angus cattle come under the scrutiny of the judges at Aberdeen Fat Stock Club Show and Sale in December 1962. The rear of the Astoria Cinema forms a backdrop to the scene, and on the left of the picture is the art deco frontage of the Northern Hotel.

This happy crowd are thoroughly enjoying themselves as they practise waving their flags minutes before the arrival of the Queen Mother to open the Beach Boulevard, near Aberdeen Beach, in May 1959.

The Queen Mother, in the back of the leading car, waves to the huge crowd which turned out to greet her when she performed the official opening of the Beach Boulevard in Aberdeen in May 1959.

The High Court sits in Aberdeen in May 1962. Presiding judge Lord Milligan inspects the guard of honour of men from the Black Watch and Argyll and Sutherland Highlanders outside Aberdeen Sheriff Court. A large crowd witnesses the historic event – the first time on record that the guard had not been composed of men of the Gordon Highlanders, because the regiment was serving in Kenya.

A radiant Queen Mother waves to the crowds in October 1966 as she leaves the Wallace Tower. The historic landmark and former pub was removed from the city centre to make way for the revamped St Nicholas Street and rebuilt on a prominent, raised site, where it became home for some years to a future Lord Provost Jim Wyness.

Crowds line the entrance to Aberdeen Station in April 1963, for the official opening of the city's new bus station in Guild Street. The ceremony was performed by Major David Gordon, later Marquess of Aberdeen.

The king is dead, long live the queen! The proclamation ceremony at Aberdeen's Castlegate in February 1952 drew large crowds to the city centre. Following the death of King George VI, Princess Elizabeth was proclaimed Queen and the town council celebrated the occasion in style. However, the day was crowned at the Town House when a table, loaded with champagne glasses, was inadvertently knocked over and dozens of glasses smashed.

A proud moment for the 4/7th Gordon Highlanders as they march down a thronged Union Street in August 1955, after receiving new colours from the Duke of Gloucester at Harlaw.

The flags and bunting are out and it's a grand day off for all school children to watch the Coronation Parade down Union Street on June 2, 1953. Baillies and other dignitaries take pride of place on the steps of the Music Hall as members of the armed forces march smartly past. Note the children, warmly wrapped against the cold wind, enjoying a grandstand view of the proceedings just to the right of the Music Hall.

The Monkey House is festooned in flowers, flags and garlands for the Coronation Parade in 1953. The crowning of Queen Elizabeth II at Westminster Abbey was greeted with a fervour in Aberdeen that we are unlikely ever to see again for a royal occasion.

This impressive shot of the Remembrance Day Parade at Aberdeen's war memorial in November 1967, was achieved by taking two pictures from the same spot and joining them in the middle. The Revd Walter J. Gordon conducts the service in front of the Lion statue.

A stunning view of the Remembrance Day Parade in Aberdeen in November 1965. And there was good reason for the photographer to get a bird's-eye view of the proceedings. It shows the readers how the Lion statue had been defaced by vandals. The picture clearly shows black writing covering the entire back of the Lion which Corporation Works Department staff were unable to clean off in time for the ceremony.

Positively gleaming – the Lord Provost's new Daimler limousine rolls into service in Aberdeen in June 1957, retaining the same number plate and civic pennant. Resplendent in his Lord Lieutenant's uniform, Lord Provost George Stephen casts an approving eye over his new civic pride and joy while Town Sergeant John Skene and chauffeur Andrew Urquhart look on admiringly.

In May 1968, the *Evening Express* turned the spotlight on the 33 men and one woman chosen by the people to guide the city's destiny. Lord Provost Robert Lennox and the new magistrates in their robes of office are seen seated with town clerk J.C. Rennie. Behind, in his robes of office is Dean of Guild J.R. Ronald, and on the far left is Senior Town Sergeant John Cowie. The lone woman is Councillor Mrs Ellen Williamson.

New Baillies being sworn into office in the council chamber at Aberdeen Town House in May 1967. Left to right are Arnold Burns, John Stephen, Alexander Mutch, Robert Robertson and Henry Hatch. Councillor Robertson would later become Lord Provost and Councillor Mutch convener of Grampian Region.

Election fever grips Aberdeen in May 1969, and the larger than life Baillie Dick Gallagher, Progressive candidate for St Nicholas ward was out in Union Street banging the drum for his party.

The 'father' of the Labour Group on Aberdeen Town council, G.R. McIntosh, finally lost his seat in May 1966, after 23 years service. As he reflected on his defeat next morning while tending his garden, the much loved 76-year-old veteran councillor, known to all as G.R., said his only real sorrow was that he would have to break the news of his defeat in the election to his wife, who was in hospital. The former joiner's other claim to fame was his coffee tables, one of which is still in daily use in my home.

Former Lord Provost of Aberdeen, W.D. Reid, was in the headlines again when he took a bride at the age of 80. The former civic head married Mrs Anne Halley of Edinburgh at Aberdeen Registrar's Office.

Aberdeen's first Socialist Lord Provost, Duncan Fraser, was made a CBE in the 1950 New Year's Honours List. Mr Fraser is pictured at his desk in June 1962, in his popular drapery shop which bore his name at the bottom of Schoolhill.

Town Sergeant Sidney Stephen leads the procession as members of Aberdeen Town Council walk through the snow in January 1965 on their way to the city's 'mither kirk', the West Church of St Nicholas, for the memorial service to Sir Winston Churchill following the death of the great statesman and Freeman of the city.

It's thumbs up for Labour in South Aberdeen in the general election of March 1966 and Donald Dewar savours his hour of victory while Lady Tweedsmuir manages to smile in the face of defeat.

The imposing figure of Town Sergeant Sidney Stephen carrying Aberdeen's mace in April 1969. The magnificent mace derives from the ancient weapon used mostly by militant churchmen. Sidney's striking red coat and white gloves depict the city's livery colours and his gold buttons show the city's coat of arms.

Pipers Ian Gray and William Donaldson from Fraserburgh lead the rectorial procession of students from Marischal College to the Blue Lamp Pub in the Gallowgate with the victor, Frank Thomson, carried shoulder high by his election supporters in February 1967. In the background, St Nicholas House, the new headquarters of Aberdeen Town Council takes shape.

As traditions go, this had to be one of the strangest for distinguished Aberdeen businessmen. Here Frank Philip of Elmfield Avenue is undergoing the 'douping' ceremony on the March Stane near Trinity Cemetery in October 1962. Eight new first masters of their trades who had entered the Convener's Court of the Incorporated Trades went through the ceremony. Frank was factor of Trinity Cemetery. The others were: J.T.L. Parkinson, of Seafield Road (Hammermen); James Duncan jnr, Hosefield Avenue (bakers); Gordon Archibald, Woodend Place (wrights and coopers); Ronald A. Murray, Fountainhall Road (tailors); Donald A. Low, Airyhall Place (shoemakers); John Scott, Woodhill Terrace (weavers); and John Farquharson, Gladstone Place (boxmaster of weavers).

Bearded millionaire tycoon Frank Thomson was chief guest of Aberdeen Junior Chamber of Commerce at their dinner in the Treetops Hotel in November 1966.

Top Aberdeen businessmen in their finery in November 1967. These are the members of the Convener Court of the Seven Incorporated Trades of Aberdeen after their election in the new Trinity Hall in Holburn Street. In front, with patron, the Revd Dr Anderson Nicol, are Mr George Gorrod, third left, deacon convener; and Mr C.A.B. Duncan, second right, Master of Hospital.

Subscribers

Alex Anderson
Alan E. Archibald
Alexander Bain
Stanley Barry
Mrs Jean Bavidge
Jim Beattie
Eileen Begg
Arthur Bertram
Stephen Booth (Oldmeldrum)
Thomas Burman
Abbie & Dorothy Carle
Richard Clark
Rowan Court
Mr Charles B. Coutts
Vi & George Cowie
G. Cruickshank
John Mcbain Cumming
Jess Cushnie
Leith Cushnie
Anne Cushnie
Brian Davidson
Dianne Davidson
Revd John Dickson
Margaret Donald
Alexander E. Donald
Robin Duncan
Ron Fiddes
Margaret & Bertie Findlay (Corby)
Gilbert Fraser
Ayleen M. Fraser
Maureen Gaskin
Mrs A. Gordon
George Gray
Charles Greig
Laraine Harris
Fiona Hendry
Hendry Hepburn
Bruce Hill
Joanne Lee Hogan
Ian Hogg
George Howie
Mike & Aileen Johnston
Alex Johnston
Kathleen Kemp
Yvonne Lane
Ronald Lawrence
Jacqueline Leith
Vivian Lennox
Frederick Thomas Lorimer

Annette M. Macdonald
William Y. Malhan
Phyllis Masson
Mrs Stella May (née Stevenson)
Gilbert Mchardy
Stella & Brian Mchardy
Brian Mcleod
Mrs Helen Moir
Arthur Murphy
Ronald Murray
Mr & Mrs M. Murray
Betty Mutch
Mr James Nicoll
Wilma Parkinson
George Paterson
Flora Rae
Miss Linda Reid
Mike Reid
Billy & Sheila Roberton
John Robertson
Scott David Robertson
Ron Robertson
Mrs Ethel Russell
Agnes & Colin Shand (New Zealand)
Isabella Shaw
Mr Donald Shaw
Mr Frank Sim
Brian Simpson
Brian Simpson
Dolina M. & Ian B. M. Skinner
Margaret S. J. Skinner
Ronald W. Smith
Helen & Norman Smith
Kevin G. Smith
Malcolm D. Smith
George Stephen
Linda Stephen
Colin Stewart
Iain A. Stuart
I. Tawse
Mr W. Tennant
Stanley Thain
Isobel Thomson
Greig Turnbull
Mabel Walker
Ian Watson
R. G. Westland
Andrew Alexander Wisely
Doris & Jim Wood
Arthur Wyllie
Rachel Macaskill Lorimer Yorston